Using the Workbook

The following conventions are used throughout this workbook:

Concept sections

Concept sections are preceded by a reading-glasses icon.

Example:  **For Your Information**

These sections are designed to be read, not keystroked.

TRY IT exercises

These exercises are designed to be keystroked, and are preceded by a keyboard icon.

- When two keys are joined by a plus sign, press the first key, and while holding it down, press the second key.

  Example: **[Ctrl] + [Home]**

- When two keys appear next to each other, press the first key, release it, then press the second key.

  Example: **[Tab] [Tab]**

- Characters to type are bolded, and keys to press are in brackets and also appear bolded.

  Examples: Type: **Office Supplies**

  Press: **[Enter]**

- Menu items and command buttons to click appear in bold.

  Examples: Click: **File** on the menu bar

  Click: the **OK** button

- Computer responses appear in italics.

  Example: *The File menu is displayed.*

WordPerfect 8.0 for Windows 95: Intermediate

Acknowledgments

This edition of the workbook is based on WordPerfect 8. Other application versions may vary.

#151 120997v1PDF

Visit our Web site at www.activeeducation.com

Course Notes

ActiveEducation Instructional Design Philosophy

ActiveEducation curriculum focuses on teaching the software skills that are essential in today's workplace. Our instructional design philosophy is to **present concepts**, provide relevant **hands-on exercises**, and then **review** those concepts. Research has proven that people learn best when a concept is presented, then practiced and reinforced. This instructional design philosophy is consistent for all ActiveEducation products, and is reflected in the way the materials are organized.

Understanding Workbook Components

Lesson Objectives — Clearly stated objectives set the expectations for each lesson, and provide a sense of accomplishment as each objective is completed.

For Your Information — Each lesson begins with an overview of the lesson content. The concepts for each lesson, along with their respective graphics, are presented. Retention is increased by previewing each technique prior to the hands-on exercise.

TRY IT exercises — Hands-on exercises are used throughout each leson and provide valuable experience with each task. TRY IT exercises reinforce the learning process and prepare the students to effectively use the software.

Lesson Summaries — Summaries are provided for additional reinforcement and retention of the major concepts and techniques learned in each lesson. Summaries also make the workbook an excellent post-training reference source by providing step-by-step instructions for each task.

Practice Exercises — Each lesson ends with a hands-on exercise that provides the students with a real-life business task to complete. The purpose of the exercise is to test and reinforce the skills and concepts learned in each lesson.

Graphics usage — ActiveEducation workbooks use graphics throughout each session to illustrate actual computer screens and icons. The use of graphics as a visual aid contributes significantly to recognizing and retaining keyboard and screen functions.

Understanding the Development Specifications

This workbook was developed with WordPerfect 8 running under Microsoft Windows 95 on a Pentium 133 Mhz computer. This system was equipped with an SVGA card and an HP LaserJet 4 printer. If you are running the program using a different hardware and/or software configuration, you may, in certain instances, obtain results that vary slightly from what is indicated in this workbook. This, however, should not affect the usefulness of the course.

Additionally, this workbook was developed under the assumption that the user will be running WordPerfect with all the default settings in effect. This is the same as running the application for the first time after installation. Also, be sure to install all of the help components.

Using the Data Files

The following files are provided on the data diskette (in compressed format) and are used during this course:

Blackbry	Review
Compnws	Smith
Format2	TURNER
JACKSON	Vendors
Jones	Work2-2
Newstyle	Work2-3
Printers	Work2-4
Register	Work2-5

To uncompress the WordPerfect 8.0 data files:

1. Insert the data diskette in drive A.
2. Use either My Computer or Windows Explorer to view the contents of the diskette in drive A.
3. Double-click the file named **wp82data.exe**.
4. When the WinZip Self Extractor dialog box appears, you may specify a folder (on your hard disk or on a network drive) where you want the data files to be located. The default extraction location is to the diskette itself (drive A).
5. Click the Unzip button to extract the files to the desired location.

You may repeat this procedure at any time to restore the data files to the original form or to extract them to another location.

Table of Contents

Lesson 4 Customizing Text and Graphics *91*

Introduction

Course Prerequisites

This course, *WordPerfect 8 for Windows 95: Intermediate*, is designed to enhance the skills acquired in WordPerfect 8 for Windows 95: Introduction. The prerequisite for this course is completion of *WordPerfect 8 for Windows 95: Introduction* or a comfortable working knowledge of basic WordPerfect operations.

Course Objectives

By the end of this course, you will be able to:

- review basic operations/work with multiple document windows
- use styles
- work with columns and tables
- customize text
- use the Merge feature
- create macros and templates

Lesson 1 Review/Working with Document Windows

Lesson Objectives

By the end of this lesson, you will have reviewed many of WordPerfect's basic operations. You will also be able to view different documents at the same time using multiple windows and copy text from one document to another.

You will learn how to:

- review basic WordPerfect operations
- display multiple document windows
- resize and reposition document windows

Reviewing Basic WordPerfect Operations

For Your Information

Before learning any new techniques, you will have an opportunity to review many of the operations presented in *WordPerfect 8 for Windows 95: Introduction.*

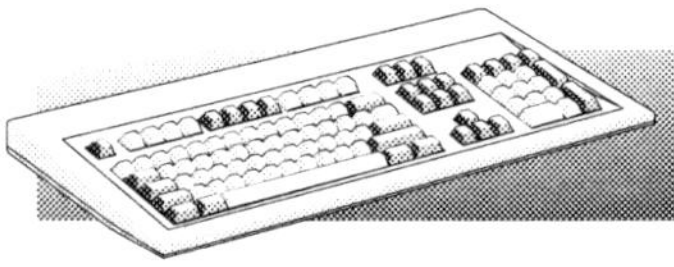

TRY IT 1–1 — Reviewing Basic WordPerfect Operations

In this exercise, you will review opening a file, changing margins, enhancing text, cutting and pasting text, setting tabs and adding text to a document, spell-checking a document, and changing justification. You will also review printing and saving a file.

NOTE: The answers to the review follow this exercise.

1. **Start WordPerfect 8 and insert your data diskette in the floppy drive.**

2. **Open the file named Review on your data diskette.**

3. **Change the left and right margins to 1.5 inches and the top margin to 2.5 inches.**

4. **Delete the second sentence in the third paragraph, which begins with "We hope."**

5. **Delete the underline in the first paragraph.**

6. **Bold the words "New York" and "Los Angeles" in the third paragraph.**

7. **Reverse the order of the second and third paragraphs.**

8. **Create a centered table between the third and fourth paragraphs containing the following list of services:**

Wills
Divorces
Criminal Cases
International Law

9. **Spell-check the document and make corrections as needed.**

10. **Change the justification of the entire document to full alignment. The completed letter should look similar to the following:**

Mr. Patrick McHenry
123 W. 45th St.
New York, NY 10007

Dear Patrick:

Thank you for your recent inquiry about our firm. We have been serving the legal needs of our neighbors for 30 years and are proud of our commitment and standing in the community.

We have 20 lawyers in our offices, both here in **New York** and in **Los Angeles**. In addition, we have associate practices in five other major cities in the United States and Europe.

In recent months, we have expanded our practice to include many new services. To date, we are providing the following legal services and advice:

Wills
Divorces
Criminal Cases
International Law

For your information, I have enclosed a list of fees for our various services. I look forward to our first meeting.

Sincerely,

Lee Galaway
Attorney at Law

Enclosure

11. **Save the file with the new filename Mchenry.**

12. **Print the file, then close the document window.**

Review Answers

1. **Start WordPerfect 8 and insert your data diskette in the floppy drive.**

    Click: the **Start** button

    Select: **Corel WordPerfect Suite 8**

    Click: **Corel WordPerfect 8**

    Next: Insert the WordPerfect data diskette in the floppy drive.

2. **Open the file named Review on your data diskette.**

    Click: the **Open** button on the toolbar

    Next: Expand the Look in drop-down list box, then click the floppy drive icon.

    Double-Click: **Review**

3. **Change the left and right margins to 1.5 inches and the top margin to 2.5 inches.**

    Click: **Format** on the menu bar

    Click: **Margins** on the Format menu

    Type: **1.5** in the Left text box

    Press: **[Tab]**

    Type: **1.5** in the Right text box

    Press: **[Tab]**

    Type: **2.5** in the Top text box

    Click: the **OK** button

4. **Delete the second sentence in the third paragraph, which begins with "We hope ..."**

First: Select the sentence.

Press: **[Delete]**

5. **Delete the underline in the first paragraph.**

First: Position the insertion point in the first paragraph.

Click: **View** on the menu bar

Click: **Reveal Codes** on the View menu

Then: Position the insertion point to the right of either Underline code.

Press: **[Backspace]**

Click: **View** on the menu bar

Click: **Reveal Codes** on the View menu

6. **Bold the words "New York" and "Los Angeles" in the third paragraph.**

First: Select "New York".

Click: the **Bold** button

Then: Select "Los Angeles".

Click: the **Bold** button

7. **Reverse the order of the second and third paragraphs.**

First: Select the third paragraph, including the blank line that follows the paragraph.

Click: the **Cut** button

Next: Move the insertion point to the beginning of the second paragraph.

Click: the **Paste** button

8. Create a centered table between the third and fourth paragraphs.

First: Position the insertion point in the blank line between the third and fourth paragraphs.

Click: **Format** on the menu bar

Select: **Line** on the Format menu

Click: **Tab Set** on the Line submenu

Click: the **Clear All** button

Then: Expand the Tab type box and select **Center**.

Next: Double-click in the Tab position text box.

Type: **2.7**

Click: the **Set** button

Click: the **OK** button

Press: **[Tab]**

Type: **Wills**

Press: **[Enter]**

Then: Type the remaining list of services using the steps above:

Divorces
Criminal Cases
International Law

9. Spell-check the document.

Click:	**Tools** on the menu bar
Click:	**Spell Check** on the Tools menu
Next:	Make corrections as needed.
Click:	the **Yes** button

10. Change the justification of the entire document to full alignment.

Press:	**[Ctrl] + [Home]**
Click:	**Format** on the menu bar
Select:	**Justification** on the Format menu
Click:	**Full** on the Justification submenu

11. Save the file with the new filename Mchenry.

Click:	**File** on the menu bar
Click:	**Save As** on the File menu
Type:	**Mchenry**
Click:	the **Save** button

12. Print the file, then close the document window.

Click:	the **Print** button
Click:	the **Print** button
Click:	**File** on the menu bar
Click:	**Close** on the File menu

Working with Multiple Document Windows

For Your Information

The Windows environment allows you to run multiple applications simultaneously, each in its own window. Similarly, WordPerfect allows you to set up multiple document windows within its application window. These windows can be used to display different parts of the same document, or they can be used to display different documents. They can also be moved, sized, and arranged to view the contents in many different ways.

Opening a New Document Window

Each new window you open in WordPerfect is displayed full-sized inside the application window and is placed on top of the current document window. To open more than one document window, select either the Open or the New command on the File menu.

Opening a Copy of a Document

Clicking the Open as copy button in the Open dialog box allows you to open a read-only copy of a document. A *read-only* copy cannot be saved over the original file. Selecting this option prevents you from accidentally saving unwanted changes to a document. This option is also useful if you wish to create a document similar to the one you have already saved to disk. You can open a copy of a document, make changes to the copy, and then save the copy with a different filename.

Activating Document Windows

The Window menu lists all document windows that are currently open and displays a checkmark next to the active window. The *active document* window is the window in which the insertion point is located, and the title bar is displayed in either a different color or a different intensity. The active document will also display the ruler bar if it is turned on.

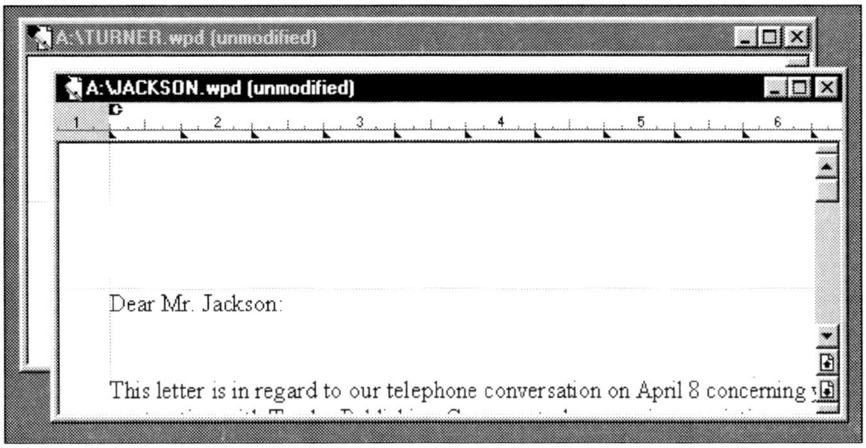

To activate a document window:

- Click Window on the menu bar.
- Click the filename of the document you wish to activate.

Using the Application Bar

Each time a document is opened, a button is displayed on the Application Bar. You can use these buttons to quickly switch between the documents you have open, as shown below:

Arranging Multiple Document Windows

WordPerfect provides two different types of window arrangements: cascading and tiled. *Cascading* windows overlap so that the title bar of each window is displayed; *tiled* windows are arranged either top-to-bottom or side-by-side with no overlapping.

To arrange document windows:

- Click Window on the menu bar.
- Click Cascade, Tile Top to Bottom, or Tile Side by Side on the Window menu.

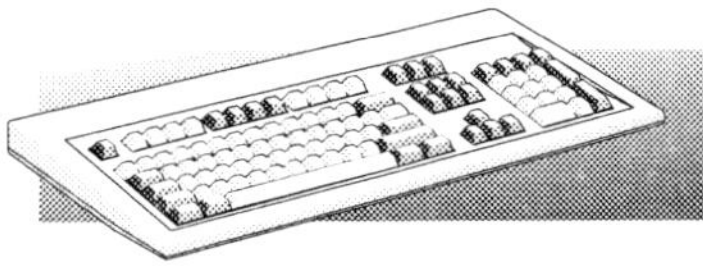

TRY IT 1–2 — Displaying Multiple Document Windows

In this exercise, you will open two document windows, move between the windows, then arrange the windows.

1. **Open two document windows.**

   Click: the **Open** button

   The Open File dialog box is displayed.

   Double-Click: **Jackson** in the file list box

   The Jackson.wpd file is displayed in the document window.

   Click: the **Open** button

   Double-Click: **Turner** in the file list box

   The Turner.wpd document window is displayed on top of the Jackson.wpd document window.

2. **Move back and forth between the two document windows.**

   Click: **Window** on the menu bar

   Click: **1 a:\Jackson.wpd** on the Window menu

   The Jackson.wpd document window is displayed.

   Click: **Window** on the menu bar

   Click: **2 a:\Turner.wpd** on the Window menu

   The Turner.wpd document window is displayed.

TIP
You can also press [Ctrl] + [F6] to switch between open document windows.

3. **Display the document windows in a cascading arrangement, then tiled side by side.**

Click: **Window** on the menu bar

Click: **Cascade** on the Window menu

The two document windows are displayed overlapping, with the title bar of each window in view. The title bar of the active window (Turner.wpd) is highlighted:

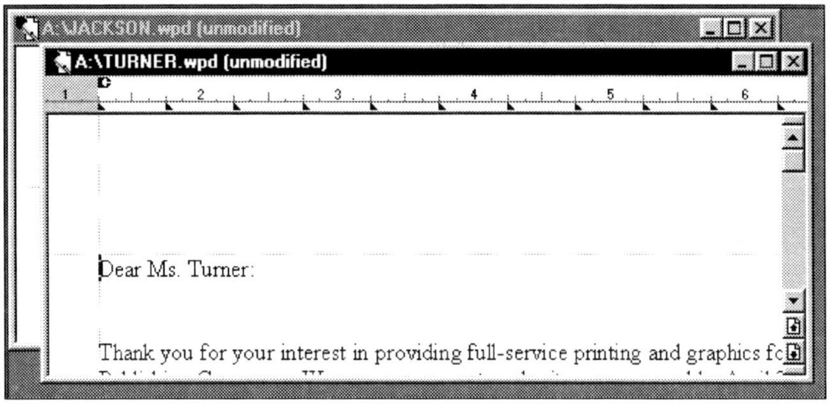

Click: **Window** on the menu bar

Click: **Tile Side by Side** on the Window menu

The two document windows are displayed with no overlapping, as displayed below:

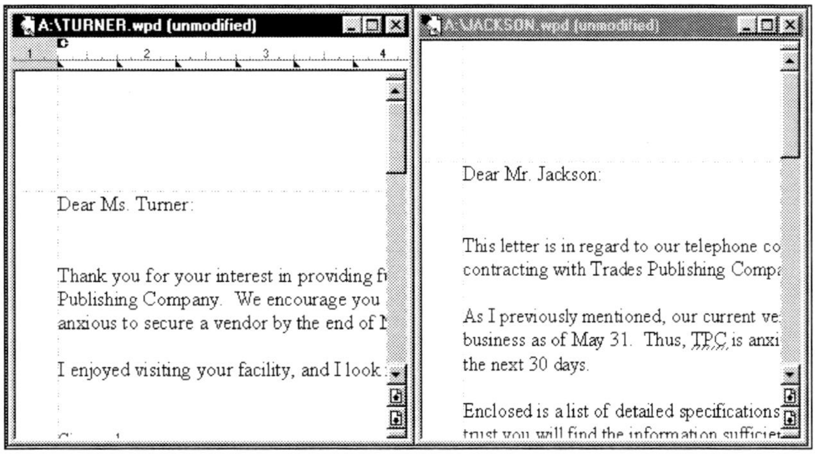

4. Copy a paragraph from Jackson.wpd to Turner.wpd.

First: In the Turner window, scroll down so that the second paragraph which begins, "I enjoyed visiting," is visible.

Next: Position the insertion point at the beginning of the second paragraph.

Then: Click anywhere in the window displaying Jackson.wpd.

The window is activated.

TIP
You can also press [Ctrl] + [C] to copy information to the clipboard.

Next: Scroll the window down so that the third paragraph which begins, "Enclosed is a list ...," is visible.

Then: Select the third paragraph, including the blank line following the paragraph.

Click: the **Copy** button

The paragraph is copied to the clipboard.

Next: Click on the blank line below the first paragraph in the window displaying Turner.wpd, and press **[Enter]**.

The left window is activated, and the insertion point is located above the second paragraph.

Click: the **Paste** button

The paragraph is inserted, and the documents should look similar to the following:

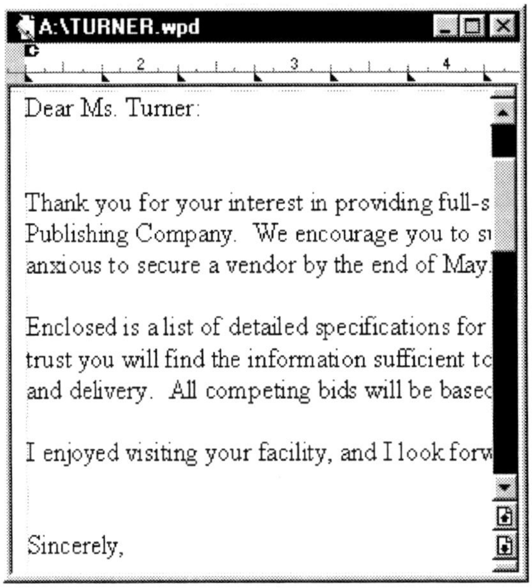

TIP
You can also press [Ctrl] + [V] to paste information from the clipboard.

5. Open a copy of Turner.wpd, then display the copy tiled with the other document windows.

Click: the **Open** button

The Open dialog box is displayed.

Click: **Turner**

Click: the **Open As copy** button

A copy of Turner.wpd is displayed on top of the other document windows.

NOTE: The title bar of the new window is marked, "Read-Only - unmodified."

Click: **Window** on the menu bar

Click: **Tile Top to Bottom** on the Window menu

The copy and the original of Turner.wpd are displayed tiled along with the Jackson.wpd document window, as displayed below:

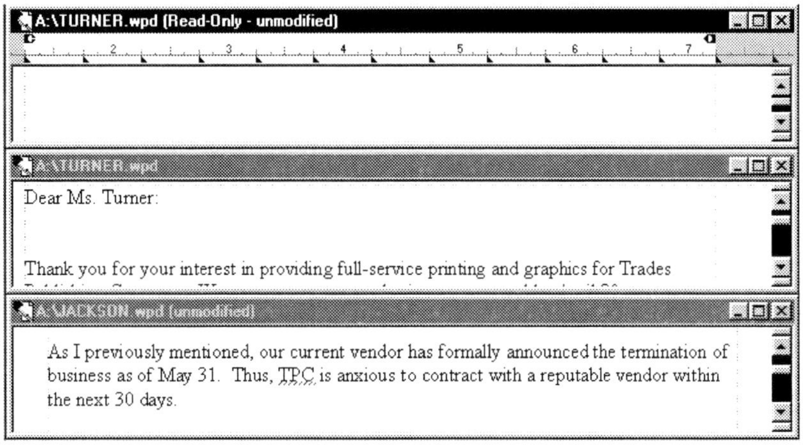

6. **Save the copy of Turner.wpd with a different filename, then close the document window.**

First: Make sure the Read Only window is active.

Click: the **Save** button

The Save As dialog box is displayed.

Type: **read only**

Click: the **Save** button

The copy is saved with a different filename.

TIP
You can also press [Ctrl] + [F4] to close an open document window.

Click: **File** on the menu bar

Click: **Close** on the File menu

The document window is closed.

7. Save the current version of Turner.wpd, then switch from one window to the other.

First: Make sure that the Turner.wpd window is active.

Click: the **Save** button

The document is saved.

Press: **[Ctrl] + [F6]**

The Jackson window is activated, and the third paragraph remains selected.

Press: **[Home]**

The paragraph is deselected.

Press: **[Ctrl] + [F6]**

The Turner window is activated.

8. On your own, redisplay the windows tiled side-by-side.

Resizing and Repositioning a Document Window

For Your Information

To help you work more efficiently with multiple documents, WordPerfect allows you to manually resize and/or reposition any open document window.

Resizing a Document Window

To resize the active document window:

- Drag the top or bottom border vertically to increase or decrease the height.
- Drag the left or right border horizontally to increase or decrease the width.
- Drag a border corner diagonally to simultaneously increase or decrease the height and width.

NOTE: The mouse pointer is displayed as a two-headed arrow when properly positioned on a window border.

Repositioning a Document Window

To reposition the active document window, simply drag the window's title bar to the desired location. The mouse pointer is displayed as a single-headed arrow when positioned on a title bar.

Maximizing and Restoring a Document Window

When working with multiple document windows, you may sometimes find it advantageous to temporarily expand a window to its full size. This can be accomplished by clicking the Maximize button in the upper-right corner of that window. Subsequently clicking the Restore button, which replaces the Maximize button when a window is expanded, restores the window to its previous size.

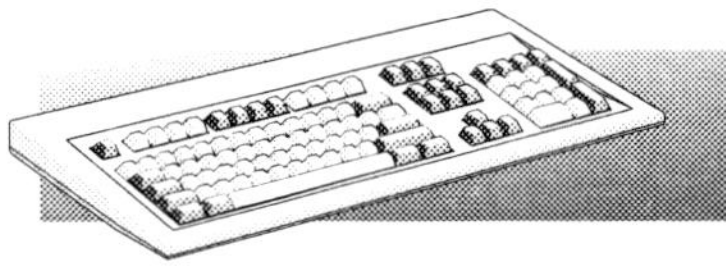

TRY IT 1-3 — Resizing and Repositioning Document Windows

In this exercise, you will open a third file. You will then resize and reposition the three document windows and maximize and restore the size of one window.

1. **On your own, open the file named Vendors.wpd.**

2. **Arrange the three open document windows so that all are displayed.**

   Click: **Window** on the menu bar

   Click: **Tile Side by Side** on the Window menu

   The document windows are displayed equally sized, one next to the other. The left window, which displays Vendors.wpd, is the active window, as displayed below:

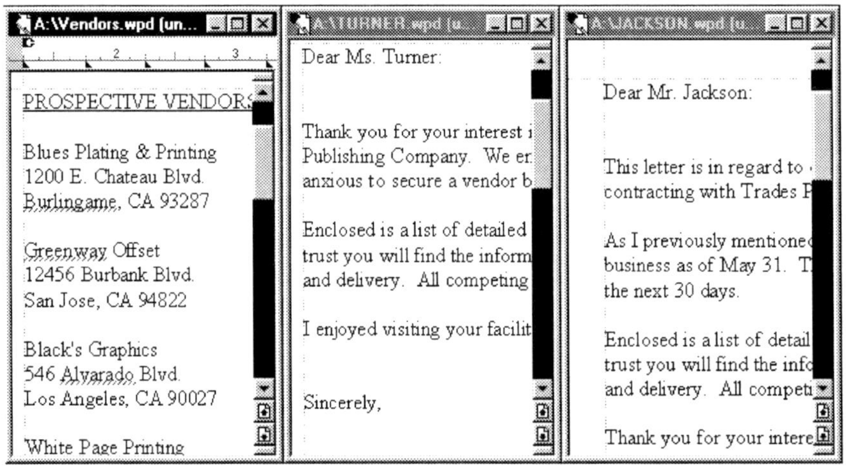

3. Resize and reposition the windows.

First:	Drag the bottom border of the window displaying Vendors.wpd approximately one-third of the way up the screen.
Next:	Drag the bottom border of the window displaying Turner.wpd approximately one-third of the way up the screen.
Then:	Drag the bottom border of the window displaying Jackson.wpd approximately two-thirds of the way up the screen.
Next:	Drag the title bar of the window displaying Jackson.wpd to the bottom-left corner of the workspace so that the window is displayed directly below the Vendors.wpd window.
Then:	Drag the right border of the window displaying Jackson.wpd to the right edge of the screen.
Next:	Drag the title bar of the window displaying Turner.wpd to the right so that the right border of the window is aligned with the right edge of the workspace.
Then:	Drag the right border of the window displaying Vendors.wpd to the midpoint of the screen, then drag the left border of the window displaying Turner.wpd to the midpoint of the screen.

The windows are resized and should look similar to the following:

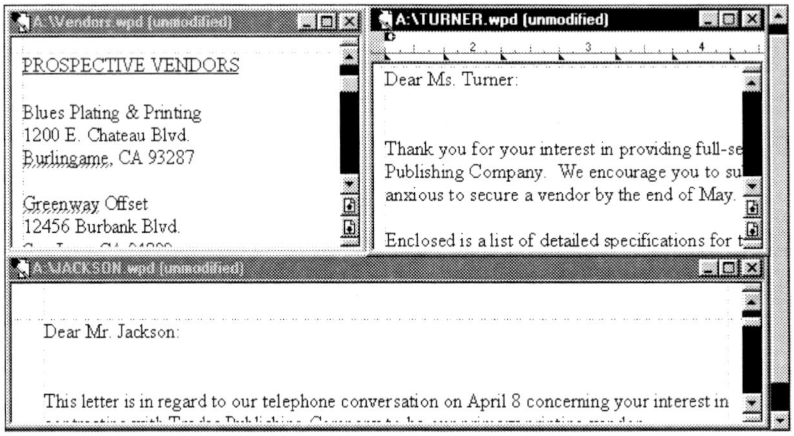

4. Maximize, then restore the active document window.

Click: the **Maximize** button of the active document window

The window is expanded to full size.

Click: the **Restore** button

The window is restored to its previous size, and all three document windows are once again displayed.

5. On your own, close all the document windows without saving.

Summary of Lesson 1

To activate a document window:

- Click **Window** on the menu bar.
- Click the filename of the document you wish to activate.

To arrange document windows:

- Click **Window** on the menu bar.
- Click **Cascade**, **Tile Top to Bottom**, or **Tile Side by Side** on the Window menu.

To resize the active document window:

- Drag the top or bottom border vertically to increase or decrease the height.
- Drag the left or right border horizontally to increase or decrease the width.
- Drag a border corner diagonally to simultaneously increase or decrease the height and width.

Practice Exercise — Lesson 1

1. Open the file named Smith on the data diskette, then open the file named Jones.

2. Display the windows first in a cascading arrangement, then in a horizontally tiles arrangement.

3. Move and resize the windows so that they appear as displayed below:

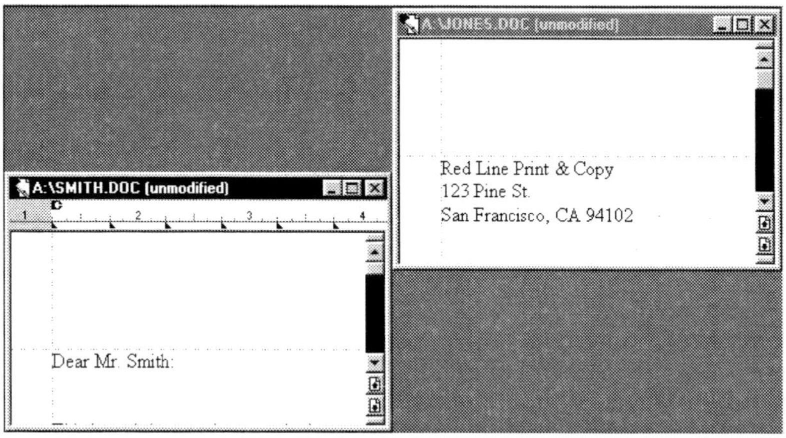

4. Copy the second and third paragraphs in the Smith document and paste them below the first paragraph in the Jones document.

5. Maximize the Jones document window, then restore the window to its original size.

6. Save both documents, then close both document windows.

Lesson 2 Using Styles

Lesson Objectives

By the end of this lesson, you will be able to automate formatting operations to create consistently formatted documents.

You will learn how to:

- create styles
- apply styles to text
- modify styles
- create a styles file

Working with Styles

For Your Information

A *style* is a named set of formatting instructions that allows you to apply multiple formatting codes to text in a single step. Styles will save you time and will help you maintain a consistent format within the same document and from document to document. There are two methods for creating a style: creating a style from scratch and basing a style on existing text.

Understanding Styles

You can create three different types of styles in WordPerfect: character, paragraph, and document. *Character* styles affect either the text you have selected or the text you are about to type. They are useful for formatting text within a paragraph. *Paragraph* styles affect the entire paragraph, with a paragraph being defined as text followed by a hard return code. Paragraph styles are useful for titles, headings, and paragraphs, as displayed below:

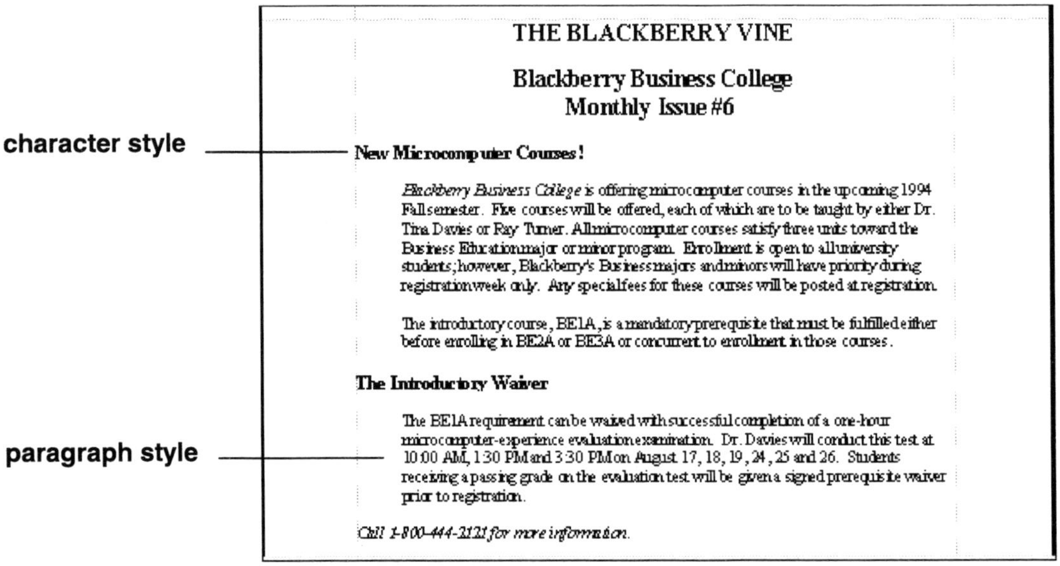

THE BLACKBERRY VINE

Blackberry Business College
Monthly Issue #6

New Microcomputer Courses!

Blackberry Business College is offering microcomputer courses in the upcoming 1994 Fall semester. Five courses will be offered, each of which are to be taught by either Dr. Tina Davies or Ray Turner. All microcomputer courses satisfy three units toward the Business Education major or minor program. Enrollment is open to all university students; however, Blackberry's Business majors and minors will have priority during registration week only. Any special fees for these courses will be posted at registration.

The introductory course, BE1A, is a mandatory prerequisite that must be fulfilled either before enrolling in BE2A or BE3A or concurrent to enrollment in those courses.

The Introductory Waiver

The BE1A requirement can be waived with successful completion of a one-hour microcomputer-experience evaluation examination. Dr. Davies will conduct this test at 10:00 AM, 1:30 PM and 3:30 PM on August 17, 18, 19, 24, 25 and 26. Students receiving a passing grade on the evaluation test will be given a signed prerequisite waiver prior to registration.

Call 1-800-444-2121 for more information.

Document styles include codes for the entire document. They are set at the beginning of a document and cannot be turned off. These styles can, however, be deleted from a document.

Creating a New Style

You begin the process of creating a new style by displaying the Styles Editor dialog box. When you create a style from scratch, you manually enter the style name and codes into the Contents box of the Styles Editor dialog box. You can use options on the Style Editor menu bar to help you enter the desired codes.

To create a style from scratch:

- Click Format on the menu bar.
- Click Styles on the Format menu.
- Click the Create button to display the following dialog box:

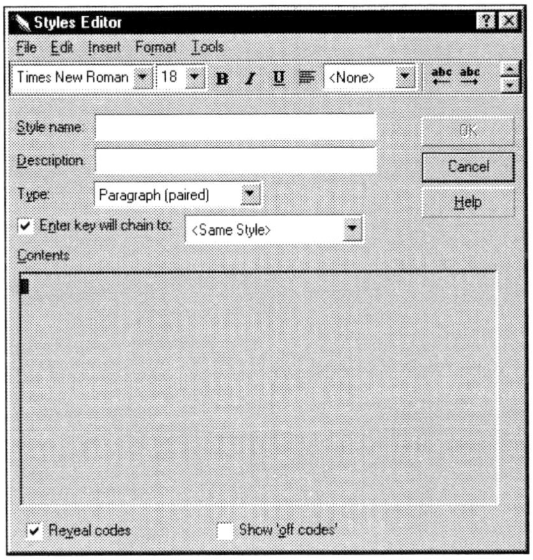

- In the Style name text box, type the name of the style.
- In the Description text box, type an optional description.
- Expand the Type list box and select a style type.
- Click in the Contents box, then enter formatting codes.
- Click the OK button.
- Click the Close button.

Creating Styles Based on Existing Text

When you create a style based on existing text, WordPerfect automatically stores the codes from the formatted text for you. You simply name the new style and give it an optional description.

To create a style from existing text:

- Position the insertion point anywhere in the formatted text.
- Click Format on the menu bar.
- Click Styles on the Format menu to display the Style List dialog box.
- Click the QuickStyle button to display the following dialog box:

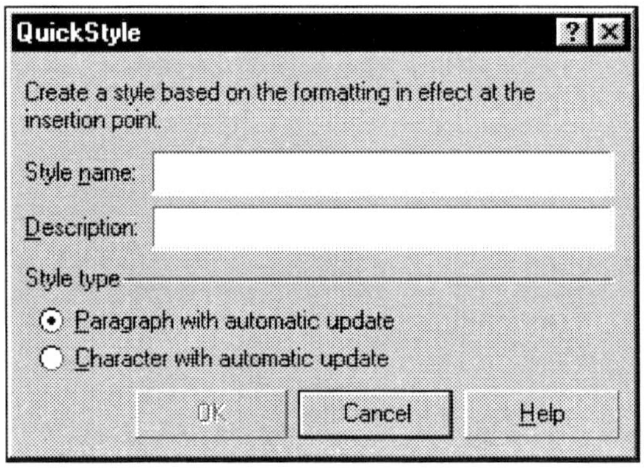

- Type a name for the style in the Style name text box.
- If desired, type a style description in the Description text box.
- Select the Style type.
- Click the OK button.
- Click the Close button.

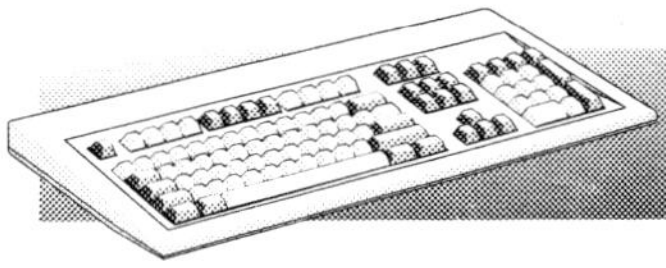

TRY IT 2-1 — Creating Styles

In this exercise, you will open a file that contains text for a newsletter. You will then create various styles.

1. On your own, open the file named Newstyle.

2. Create a paragraph style for a title. Begin by naming the style.

TIP
You can also press [Alt] + [F8] to display the Style List dialog box.

Click: **Format** on the menu bar

Click: **Styles** on the Format menu

The Style List dialog box is displayed, as follows:

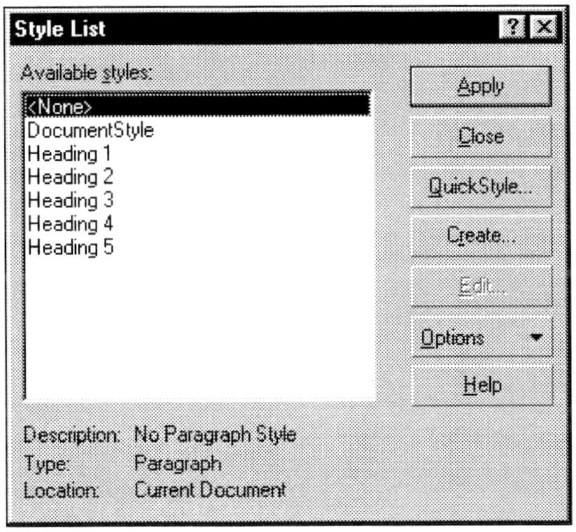

Click: the **Create** button

The Styles Editor dialog box is displayed, as follows:

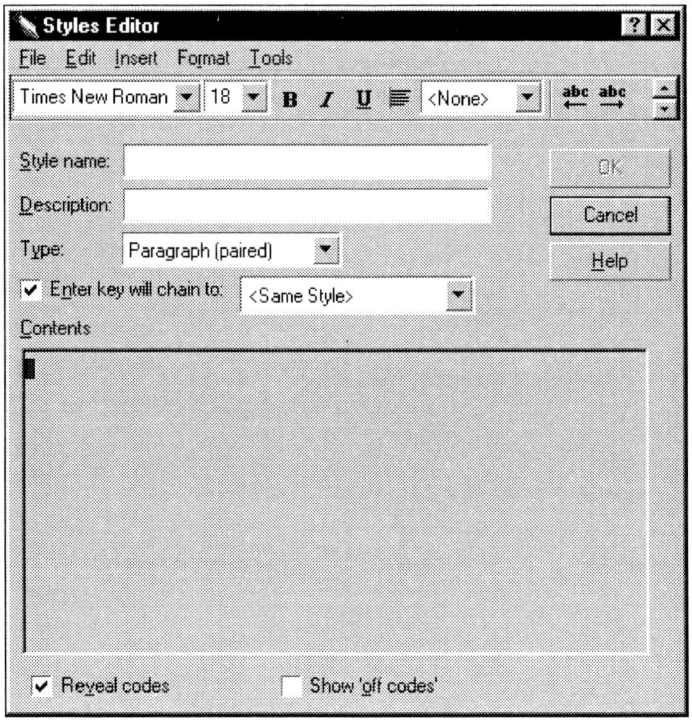

Type: **Title2** in the Style name text box

Press: **[Tab]**

Type: **Secondary title** in the Description text box

The name and description for the style are entered.

3. Enter the style formatting codes.

First: Click in the Contents box.

The Contents box is activated.

Click: **Format** on the Styles Editor menu bar

Click: **Font** on the Format menu

The Font dialog box is displayed.

Next: Click **Bold** in the Appearance section.

Then: Click **14** in the Font size list box.

Click: the **OK** button

A font size code of 14 and a bold code are inserted in the Contents box, and the dialog box should look similar to the following:

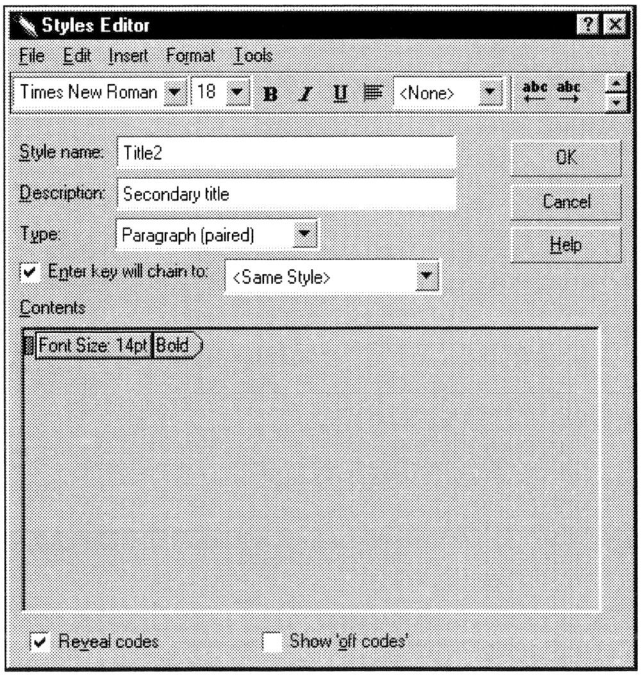

Click: the **OK** button

The paragraph style Title2 is displayed in the Available styles list box.

Click: the **Close** button

The Style List dialog box is removed.

4. Create a paragraph style for indented text.

Click: **Format** on the menu bar

Click: **Styles** on the Format menu

Click: the **Create** button

The Styles Editor dialog box is displayed.

Type: **Para1** in the Style name text box

Press: **[Tab]**

Type: **Paragraph style** in the Description text box

The style is named.

Next: Click in the Contents box.

The Contents box is activated.

Click: **Format** on the Styles Editor menu bar

Select: **Paragraph** on the Format menu

Click: **Indent** on the Paragraph submenu

An indent code is inserted in the Contents box, and the dialog box should look similar to the following:

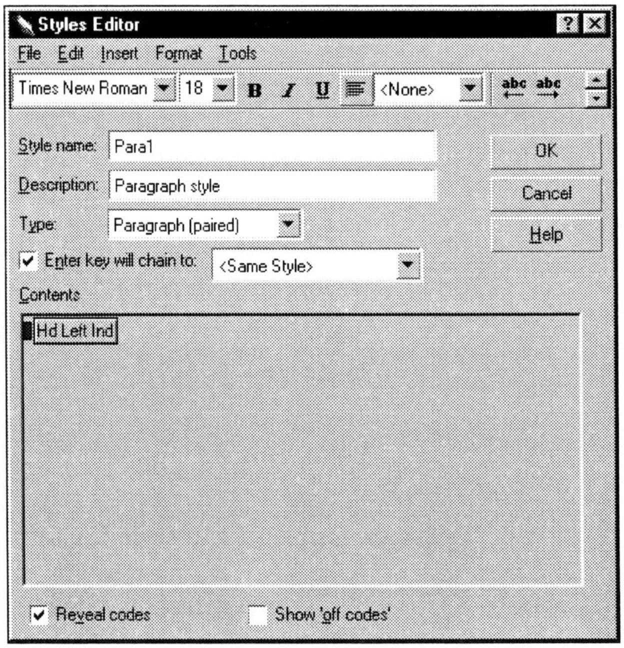

Click: the **OK** button

The paragraph style Para1 is displayed in the Available styles list box.

Click: the **Close** button

The Style List dialog box is closed.

5. Define a character style for bold and italic text.

Click: **Format** on the menu bar

Click: **Styles** on the Format menu

Click: the **Create** button

The Styles Editor dialog box is displayed.

Type: **Boldital**

Press: **[Tab]**

Type: **Bold and italic text**

A name and a description for the style are entered.

Next: Expand the Type drop-down list box, then select **Character (paired)**.

TIP
You can also use the property bar buttons to apply format to a style.

The style type is changed to Character, and the Contents box is activated.

Press: **[Ctrl] + I**

Press: **[Ctrl] + B**

Italic and bold codes are inserted, and the dialog box should look similar to the following:

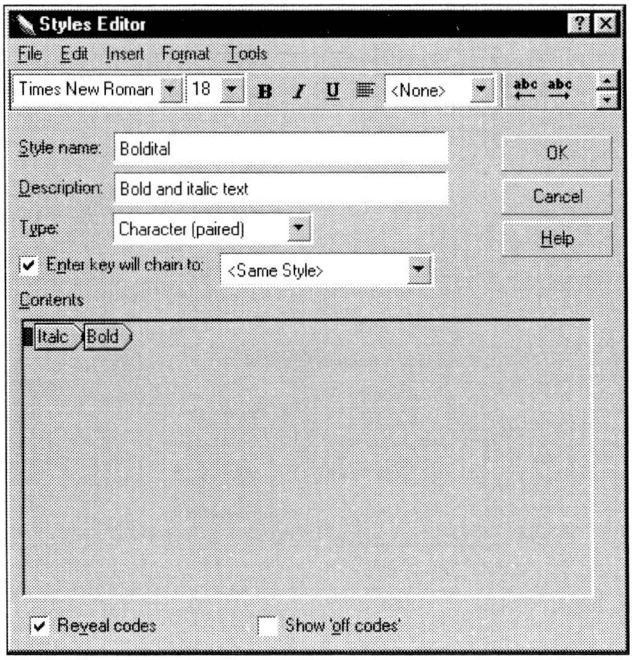

Click: the **OK** button

The style name Boldital is displayed in the Available styles list box.

Click: the **Close** button

6. Define a paragraph style based on existing text.

First: Position the insertion point anywhere in the title, "THE BLACKBERRY VINE."

Click: **Format** on the menu bar

Click: **Styles** on the Format menu

Click: the **QuickStyle** button

The QuickStyle dialog box is displayed, as follows:

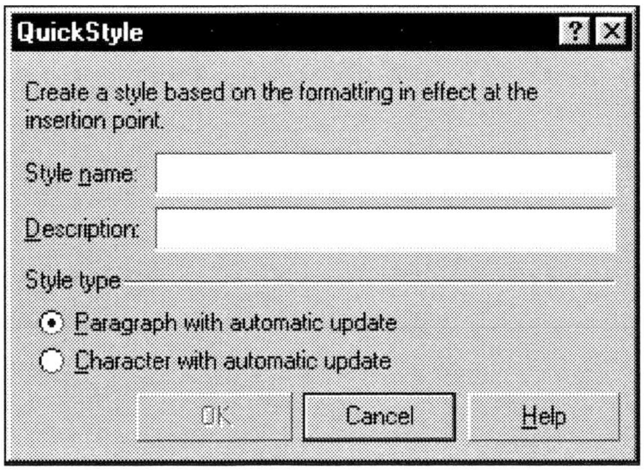

Type: **Title** in the Style name text box

Click: the **OK** button

A style is created using the existing format of the title.

7. View the codes for the Title style you just created.

First: Make sure Title is selected in the Name list box.

Click: the **Edit** button

The Styles Editor dialog box is displayed. The codes for the Title style are displayed in the Contents box and should look similar to the following:

Click: the **OK** button

Click: the **Close** button

The dialog boxes are removed.

Applying Styles

For Your Information

Once a style has been created, the *style type* determines how you apply it to text. To apply paragraph styles, you position the insertion point anywhere in the existing text, then apply the style. To apply character styles, you can either select the text you want to affect or turn the style on before typing the associated text. You can also use the QuickFormat feature to apply styles to nonconsecutive groups of text.

Applying Paragraph Styles

To apply a paragraph style to one paragraph only, you simply position the insertion point anywhere in the paragraph and apply the style. The style affects existing text up to the first hard return code. To apply the style to several paragraphs, you must select the text before applying the style.

To apply paragraph styles, position the insertion point anywhere in the text, then click Styles on the Format menu. In the Available styles list box, click the style you wish to apply, then click the Apply button.

Applying Character Styles

When a character style is applied to selected text, the text is instantly formatted according to the Contents box formatting codes. When you turn on a character style, the text is formatted as it is typed. One method for applying styles is to click the Select Style button on the property bar, then select the desired style.

To apply character styles:

- Click Styles on the Format menu.
- In the Available styles list box, select the style you wish to turn on, then click the Apply button.

You can turn off a character style either by pressing the right arrow until you move past the style code, or by applying the <None> style. You can also turn off the style by selecting <None> in the Chain to drop-down list box when creating the style.

Using QuickFormat

Using the *QuickFormat* feature, you can copy paragraph styles to non-consecutive paragraphs. You access QuickFormat by clicking the QuickFormat button on the toolbar, or by clicking QuickFormat on the Format menu.

To use QuickFormat:

- Format the paragraph with the desired style, then position the insertion point anywhere in the formatted paragraph.
- Click the QuickFormat button on the toolbar to display the following:

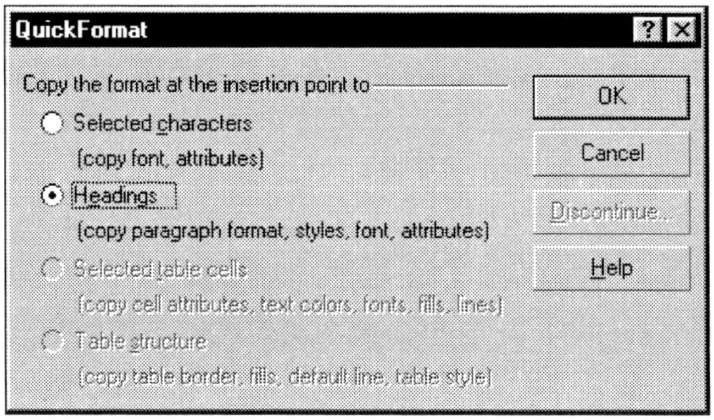

- Click Selected characters (copy font, attributes); click Headings (copy paragraph format, styles, font, attributes).
- Click the OK button.

NOTE: The insertion point is displayed with a paint roller when QuickFormat is activated.

- Drag the insertion point over the text to be formatted.
- Click the QuickFormat button on the toolbar.

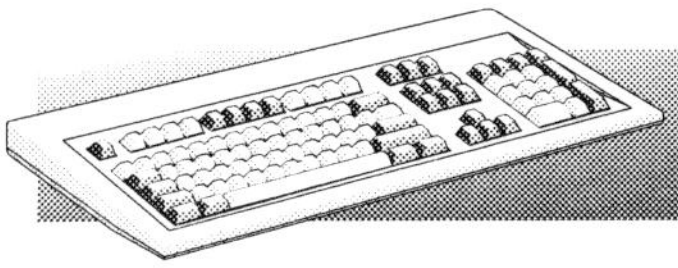

TRY IT 2–2 — Applying Styles to Text

In this exercise, you will apply the styles you have created to the current document.

1. Apply the Title style to the second line of the title.

First: Position the insertion point in the title, "Blackberry Business College."

Click: **Format** on the menu bar

Click: **Styles** on the Format menu

TIP
A style can be applied within the Style List box by double-clicking on it.

The Style List dialog box is displayed.

Click: **Title** in the Available styles list box

Click: the **Apply** button

The text is formatted according to the Title style codes and should look similar to the following:

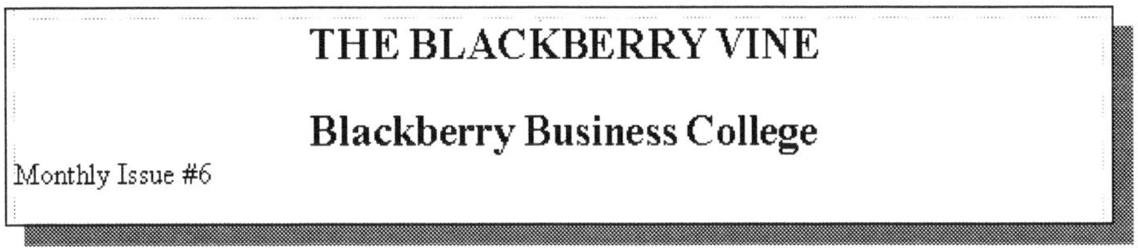
THE BLACKBERRY VINE

Blackberry Business College

Monthly Issue #6

2. **Format the third line of the title using QuickFormat.**

First: Make sure the insertion point is still positioned in the title, "Blackberry Business College."

Click: the **QuickFormat** button  on the toolbar

The QuickFormat dialog box is displayed, and Headings is selected by default, as displayed below:

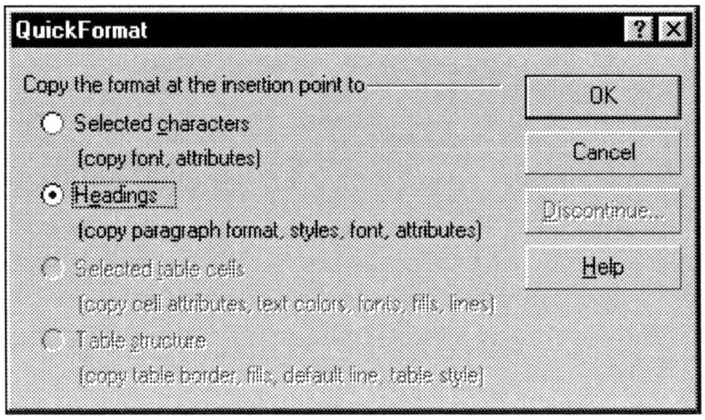

TIP
You can also access the QuickFormat command by clicking the right mouse button and selecting it from the shortcut menu while the pointer is positioned in the paragraph containing the formats to be copied.

Click: the **OK** button

The insertion point is displayed with a paint roller.

Next: Drag the insertion point over the third line of the title, "Monthly Issue #6."

The text is formatted with the Title paragraph style.

Click: the **QuickFormat** button on the toolbar

QuickFormat is turned off.

3. **Apply the Para1 style to the first paragraph.**

First:	Position the insertion point in the paragraph beginning, "Blackberry Business College is offering."
Click:	**Format** on the menu bar
Click:	**Styles** on the Format menu
Click:	**Para1** in the Name list box
Click:	the **Apply** button

The paragraph is formatted according to the Para1 style codes.

4. **On your own, apply the Para1 style to the two remaining paragraphs.**

5. **Apply the Boldital style to selected text.**

First:	Select the text, "Blackberry Business College" in the first paragraph.
Click:	the **Select Style** drop-down list box on the property bar

The Select Style drop-down list is expanded.

Click:	**Boldital**

The text is formatted according to the codes in the Boldital style.

Press:	**[Home]**

The text is deselected and should look similar to the following:

> New Microcomputer Courses!
>
> ***Blackberry Business College*** is offering microcomputer courses in the upcoming 1994 Fall semester. Five courses will be offered, each of which are to be taught by either Dr. Tina Davies or Ray Turner. All microcomputer courses satisfy three units toward the Business Education major or minor program. Enrollment is open to all university students; however, Blackberry's Business majors and minors will have priority during registration week only. Any special fees for these courses will be posted at registration.

6. Turn on a style and type text. Begin by positioning the insertion point at the end of the document.

Press: **[Ctrl] + [End]**

Click: the **Select Style** drop-down list box on the property bar

Click: **Boldital**

The style is turned on.

Type: **Call 1-800-444-2121 for more information.**

The text is formatted as it is typed.

Click: the **Select Style** drop-down list box

Click: **<None>**

The style is turned off.

7. Format the secondary titles.

First: Position the insertion point in the title, "New Microcomputer Courses!"

Click: the **Select Style** drop-down list box

Click: **Title2**

The Title2 style is applied to the title.

Next: Position the insertion point in the title, "The Introductory Waiver."

Click: the **Select Style** drop-down list box

Click: **Title2**

The Title2 style is applied to the title, and the document should look similar to the following:

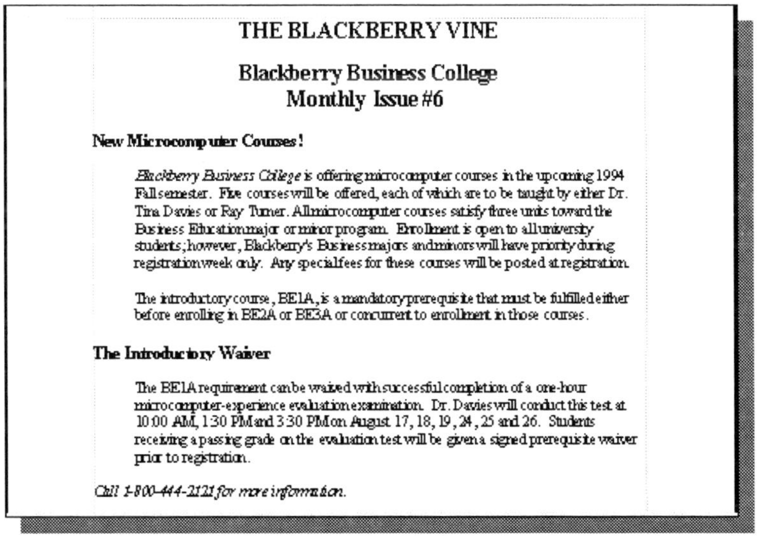
THE BLACKBERRY VINE

Blackberry Business College
Monthly Issue #6

New Microcomputer Courses!

Blackberry Business College is offering microcomputer courses in the upcoming 1994 Fall semester. Five courses will be offered, each of which are to be taught by either Dr. Tina Davies or Ray Turner. All microcomputer courses satisfy three units toward the Business Education major or minor program. Enrollment is open to all university students; however, Blackberry's Business majors and minors will have priority during registration week only. Any special fees for these courses will be posted at registration.

The introductory course, BE1A, is a mandatory prerequisite that must be fulfilled either before enrolling in BE2A or BE3A or concurrent to enrollment in those courses.

The Introductory Waiver

The BE1A requirement can be waived with successful completion of a one-hour microcomputer-experience evaluation examination. Dr. Davies will conduct this test at 10:00 AM, 1:30 PM and 3:30 PM on August 17, 18, 19, 24, 25 and 26. Students receiving a passing grade on the evaluation test will be given a signed prerequisite waiver prior to registration.

Call 1-800-444-2121 for more information.

NOTE: The document is displayed in 65% view mode to view the entire document.

8. On your own, save the current version of the document.

Modifying Styles

For Your Information

If you use styles to format the text in your document, you can easily modify the text by editing the styles. You can also completely delete the styles from the document, with the option of deleting the corresponding codes.

Editing Styles

One of the advantages of using styles to format a document is that if you decide you want to change the format of specific text in the document, you do not have to manually edit the text—you simply edit the style. When you edit a style, the changes automatically affect all text to which that style has been applied.

To edit a style, display the Style List dialog box, then select the style you wish to edit. Click the Edit button, activate the Contents box, and delete or insert the new formatting codes as desired.

Deleting Styles

You have two options when deleting a style from a document. You can delete all occurrences of the style and remove the formatting codes, or you can delete the style and leave the codes in the text.

To delete a style:

- In Style List dialog box, select the style you wish to delete.
- Click the Options button.
- Click Delete on the expanded Options list.
- Click Including formatting codes to remove the formatting codes along with the style; click Leave formatting codes in document to leave the codes in the text.
- Click the OK button.

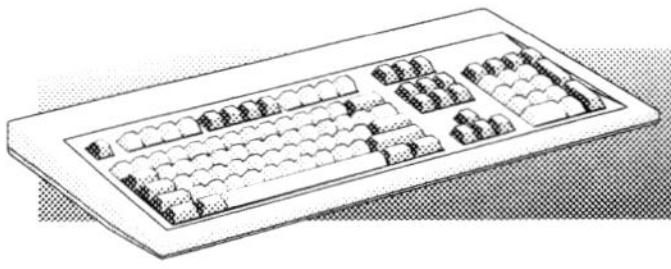

TRY IT 2-3 — Modifying Styles

In this exercise, you will edit and delete styles.

1. Edit the Title2 style. Begin by displaying the current codes in the Contents box.

Click: **Format** on the menu bar

Click: **Styles** on the Format menu

Click: **Title2** in the Available styles list box

Click: the **Edit** button

The Styles Editor dialog box is displayed with the Title2 formatting codes listed in the Contents box.

2. Change the font code for the Title2 style.

First: In the Contents box, double-click the Font Size: **14pt** code.

The Font dialog box is displayed.

Click: **16** in the Font size list box

Click: **Italic** in the Font style section

Click: the **OK** button

The new font codes are displayed in the Contents box, as displayed below:

Click: the **OK** button

Click: the **Close** button

The text previously formatted with the Title2 style is automatically updated with the new formatting codes, as displayed below:

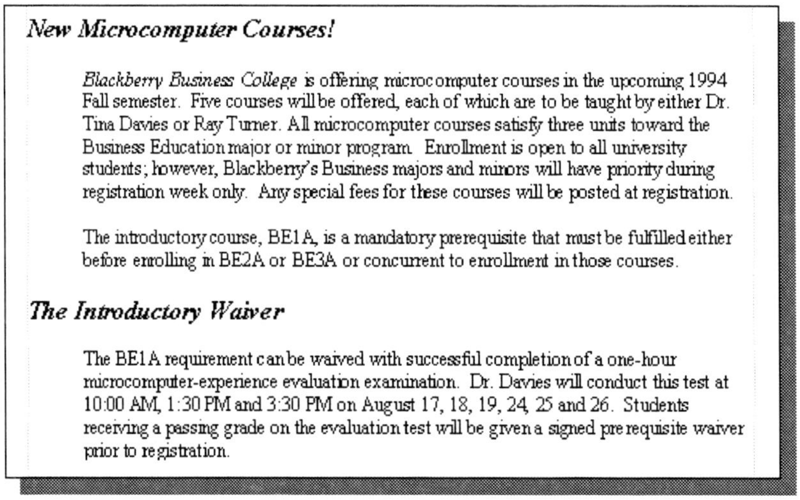

New Microcomputer Courses!

Blackberry Business College is offering microcomputer courses in the upcoming 1994 Fall semester. Five courses will be offered, each of which are to be taught by either Dr. Tina Davies or Ray Turner. All microcomputer courses satisfy three units toward the Business Education major or minor program. Enrollment is open to all university students; however, Blackberry's Business majors and minors will have priority during registration week only. Any special fees for these courses will be posted at registration.

The introductory course, BE1A, is a mandatory prerequisite that must be fulfilled either before enrolling in BE2A or BE3A or concurrent to enrollment in those courses.

The Introductory Waiver

The BE1A requirement can be waived with successful completion of a one-hour microcomputer-experience evaluation examination. Dr. Davies will conduct this test at 10:00 AM, 1:30 PM and 3:30 PM on August 17, 18, 19, 24, 25 and 26. Students receiving a passing grade on the evaluation test will be given a signed prerequisite waiver prior to registration.

3. **Edit the Para1 style to include a double indent instead of a left indent.**

Click: **Format** on the menu bar

Click: **Styles** on the Format menu

Click: **Para1** in the Name list box

Click: the **Edit** button

The Styles Editor dialog box is displayed.

Press: **[Delete]**

The Indent code is removed.

Click: **Format** on the Styles Editor menu bar

Select: **Paragraph** on the Format menu

Click: **Double Indent**

A double indent code is inserted.

Click: the **OK** button

Click: the **Close** button

The text previously formatted with the Para1 style is automatically displayed with the new formatting codes.

4. **Delete a style.**

Click: **Format** on the menu bar

Click: **Styles** on the Format menu

Click: **Title** in the Available styles list box

Click: the **Options** button in the Style List dialog box

The Options list is expanded.

Click: **Delete**

The Delete Styles dialog box is displayed, as follows:

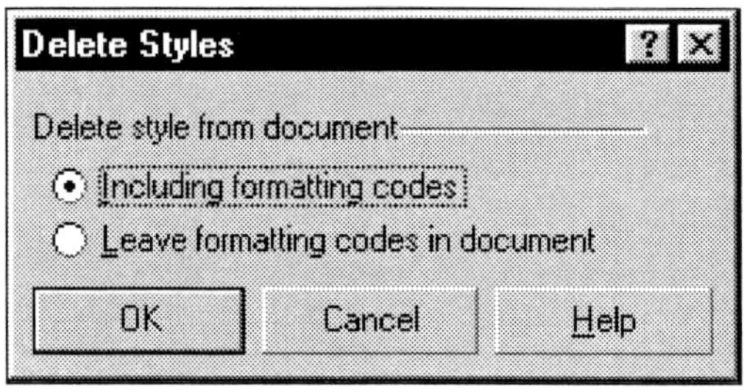

Click: **Leave formatting codes in document**

Click: the **OK** button

The Title style is deleted and is no longer displayed in the Available styles list box.

Click: the **Close** button

The dialog box is closed, and the text in the document remains formatted.

5. On your own, save the current version of the file.

Saving and Retrieving Styles

For Your Information

By default, WordPerfect stores the styles you create with the document in which you created them. For example, the styles that you created in the previous exercise are stored in the Newstyle file. To use these styles in other documents, you must first save them in a separate file.

Saving Styles in a Separate File

You save styles in a separate file using the Options button in the Style List dialog box.

To save styles in a separate file:

- Display the Style List dialog box.
- Click the Options button.
- Click Save As on the expanded Options list to display the following:

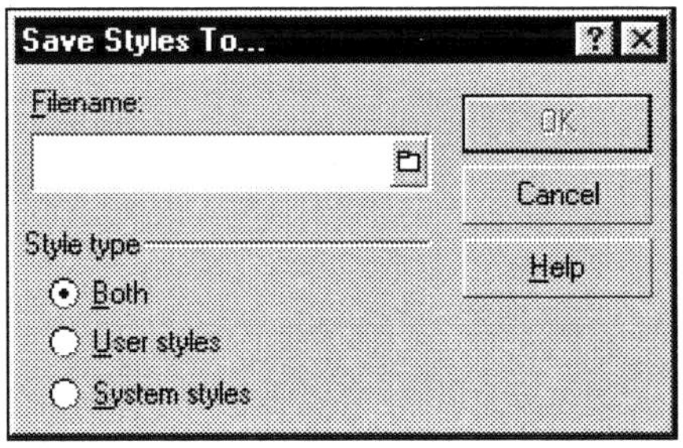

- Type a filename in the Filename text box.
- Click User styles in the Style type section to save only the styles you have created. Click System styles to save the default WordPerfect styles. Click Both to save both types of styles.
- Click the OK button.
- Click the Close button.

Retrieving Styles

You can retrieve a styles file into a new document using the Options button in the Style List dialog box. Once the file has been retrieved, you apply styles as described previously in this lesson.

To retrieve styles into a document:

- Display the Style List dialog box.
- Click the Options button.
- Click Retrieve on the expanded Options list to display the following:

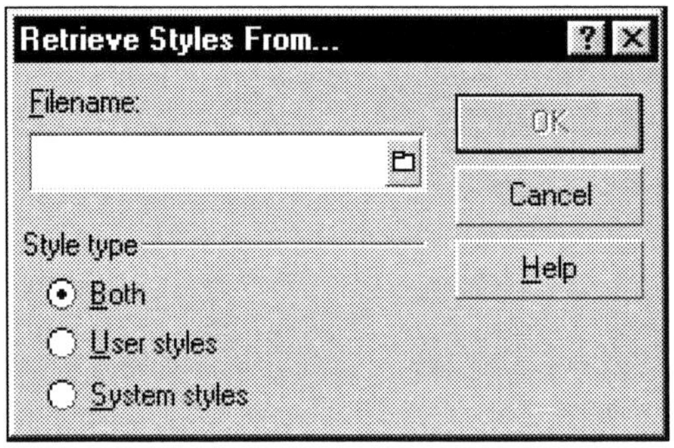

- Type a filename in the Filename text box.
- Select User styles in the Style type section to retrieve only the styles you created. Click System styles to retrieve the default WordPerfect styles. Click Both to retrieve both types of styles.
- Click the OK button.
- Click the Close button.

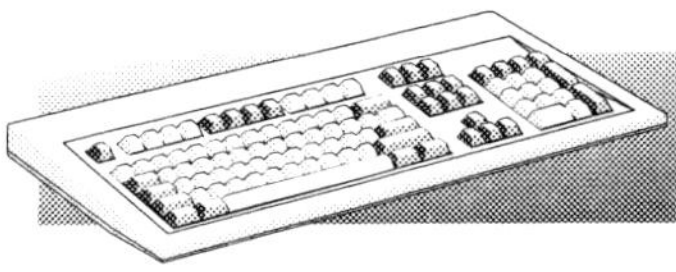

TRY IT 2-4 — Creating a Styles File

In this exercise, you will save the styles you created to a separate file, then retrieve the file into another document.

1. Save the styles created in Newstyle to a separate file.

Click: **Format** on the menu bar

Click: **Styles** on the Format menu

The Style List dialog box is displayed.

Click: the **Options** button

The Options list is expanded.

Click: **Save As** on the expanded Options list

The Save Styles To dialog box is displayed, as follows:

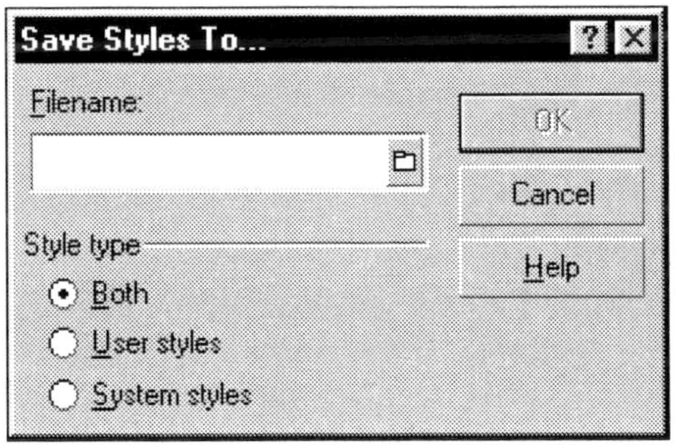

Type: **a:\newslet.sty** in the Filename text box

Next: Click **User styles** in the Style type section.

Click: the **OK** button

The styles are saved to a separate file.

Click: the **Close** button

2. **On your own, save, then close the current document.**

3. **Retrieve the styles file into a new document window.**

Click: **Format** on the menu bar

Click: **Styles** on the Format menu

The Style List dialog box is displayed.

Click: the **Options** button

The Options list is expanded.

Click: **Retrieve** on the expanded Options list

The Retrieve Styles From dialog box is displayed, as follows:

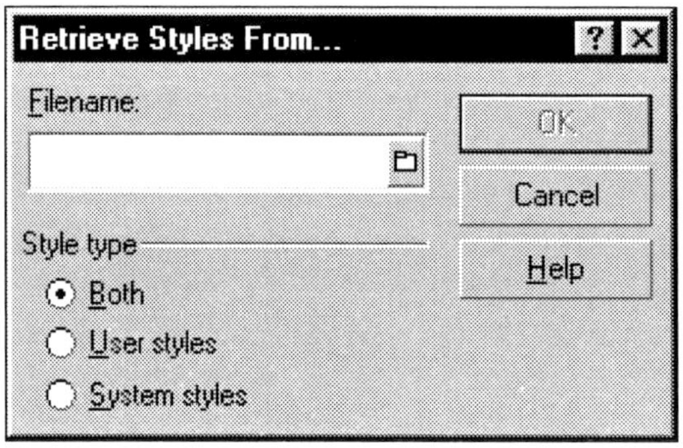

Type: **a:\newslet.sty** in the Filename text box

Click: the **OK** button

The styles are retrieved, and the style names are displayed in the Name list box, as displayed below:

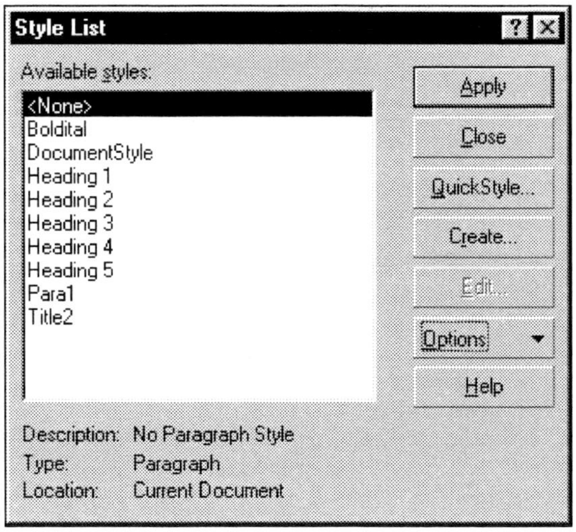

Click: the **Close** button

4. On your own, close the current document without saving.

Summary of Lesson 2

To create a style from scratch:

- Click **Format** on the menu bar.
- Click **Styles** on the Format menu.
- Click the **Create** button.
- In the Style name text box, type the name of the style.
- In the Description text box, type an optional description.
- Expand the Type list box and select a style type.
- Click in the Contents box, then enter formatting codes.
- Click the **OK** button.
- Click the **Close** button.

To create a style from existing text:

- Position the insertion point anywhere in the formatted text.
- Click **Format** on the menu bar.
- Click **Styles** on the Format menu.
- Click the **QuickStyle** button.
- Type a name for the style in the Style name text box.
- If desired, type a style description in the Description text box.
- Click the **OK** button.
- Click the **Close** button.

To apply character styles:

- Click **Format** on the menu bar.
- Click **Styles** on the Format menu.
- In the Available styles list box, select the style you wish to turn on, then click the **Apply** button.
- Type the text, then press **[Enter]**.

To use QuickFormat:

- Format the paragraph with the desired style, then position the insertion point anywhere in the formatted paragraph.
- Click the **QuickFormat** button on the toolbar.
- Click **Selected characters** (copy font, attributes); click **Headings** (copy paragraph format, styles, font, attributes).
- Click the **OK** button.
- Drag the insertion point over the text to be formatted.
- Click the **QuickFormat** button on the toolbar.

To delete a style:

- Display the Style List dialog box, then select the style you wish to delete.
- Click the **Options** button.
- Click **Delete** on the expanded Options list.
- Click **Including formatting codes** to remove the formatting codes along with the style; click **Leave formatting codes in document** to leave the codes in the text.
- Click the **OK** button.
- Click the **Close** button.

To save styles in a separate file:

- Display the Style List dialog box.
- Click the **Options** button.
- Click **Save As** on the expanded Options list.
- Type a filename in the Filename text box.
- Click **User styles** in the Style type section to save only the styles you have created. Click **System styles** to save the default WordPerfect styles. Click **Both** to save both types of styles.
- Click the **OK** button.
- Click the **Close** button.

To retrieve styles into a document:

- Display the Style List dialog box.
- Click the **Options** button.
- Click **Retrieve** on the expanded Options list.
- Type a filename in the Filename text box.
- Select **User styles** in the Style type section to retrieve only the styles you created. Click **System styles** to retrieve the default WordPerfect styles. Click **Both** to retrieve both types of styles.
- Click the **OK** button.
- Click the **Close** button.

Practice Exercise — Lesson 2

1. Open the file named Work2-2.

2. Create a style named "Heading" using the formatting characteristics of the title, "THE BLACKBERRY VINE."

3. Create a paragraph style named "Text" with full justification and a double indent.

4. Apply the Heading style to the three left-aligned titles, and the Text style to the two paragraphs. The document should look similar to the following:

> THE BLACKBERRY VINE
>
> **Blackberry Business College**
> **Monthly Issue #9**
>
> **Advanced Microcomputer Courses!**
>
> Blackberry Business College is offering advanced microcomputer courses in the upcoming 1994 Spring semester. Two courses will be offered; Advanced Database concepts and Advanced Desktop Publishing concepts.
>
> Enrollment is open to all university students; however, Blackberry's Business majors and minors will have priority during registration week only. Any special fees for these courses will be posted at registration.

5. Save and close the document.

Lesson 3 Working with Columns and Tables

Lesson Objectives

By the end of this lesson, you will be able to define and format newspaper columns. You will also be able to create and format tables and calculate data in tables.

You will learn how to:

- define columns
- customize the column format
- create a table
- modify a table
- create table formulas

Creating Newspaper Columns

For Your Information

When creating a document that requires a column format, you can select from four different column types. You create columns by first defining the column format, then typing in the desired text.

Setting Up Newspaper Columns

WordPerfect provides four different column formats: newspaper, balanced newspaper, parallel, and parallel with block protect. You use *newspaper* when you want text to flow from the bottom of one column to the top of the next. You use *balanced newspaper* when you want columns to be equal in length, as displayed below:

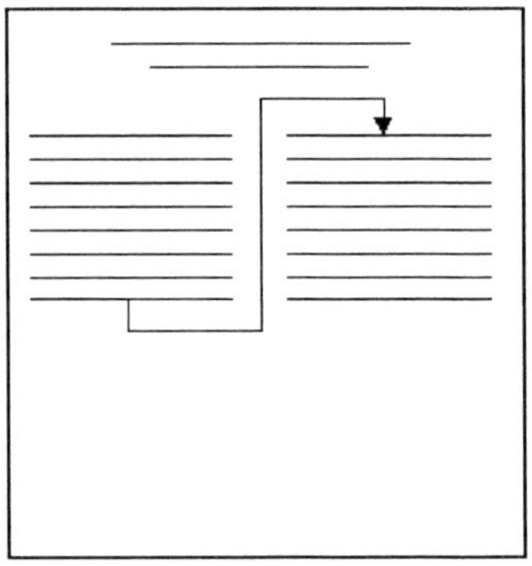

newspaper

balanced newspaper

You create *parallel* columns when you want to align text in the left column with text in the right column, while *parallel columns with block protect* keeps all rows of the columns together across page breaks. The first step in setting up columns is planning the overall layout. To do this, you determine:

- the number of columns that are to appear across the page.
- the number of lines that are to be included in each column.
- whether the columns will be regular, balanced, or parallel.

Creating Columns

When you define a column format, by default, column guidelines are displayed surrounding each column. Guidelines display as different colored lines indicating the column margins. You define columns using the Columns command on the Format menu.

To define columns:

- Position the insertion point where you want the columns to begin.
- Click Format on the menu bar.
- Click Columns on the Format menu to display the Columns dialog box.
- Type the number of columns desired in the Number of columns text box.
- Select the type of column in the Type of columns section.
- Click the OK button.

Moving Between Columns

If columns are defined in existing text, WordPerfect displays the text in the format defined. If you define columns in a blank window, any subsequent text you type will display in the format defined. You can move from column to column using either the mouse or the keyboard. To move using the mouse, simply position the insertion point and click.

To move from column to column using the keyboard, use the methods summarized below:

Press:	To go:
[Alt] + [Home]	to the top of a column
[Alt] + [End]	to the last line of a column
[Alt] + [Left Arrow]	to the previous column
[Alt] + [Right Arrow]	to the next column

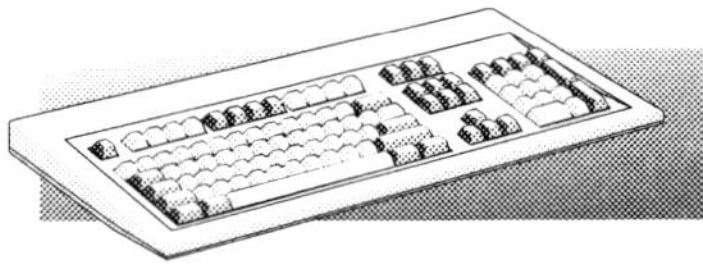

TRY IT 3–1 — Defining Columns

In this exercise, you will create a multiple-column document, then practice moving the insertion point from column to column.

1. **On your own, open the file named Blackbry.**

2. **Define a three-column balanced newspaper-style format.**

TIP
You can create and format columns using the Columns button on the toolbar.

First: Position the insertion point before the title, "New Microcomputer Courses."

Click: **Format** on the menu bar

Click: **Columns** on the Format menu

The Columns dialog box is displayed, as follows:

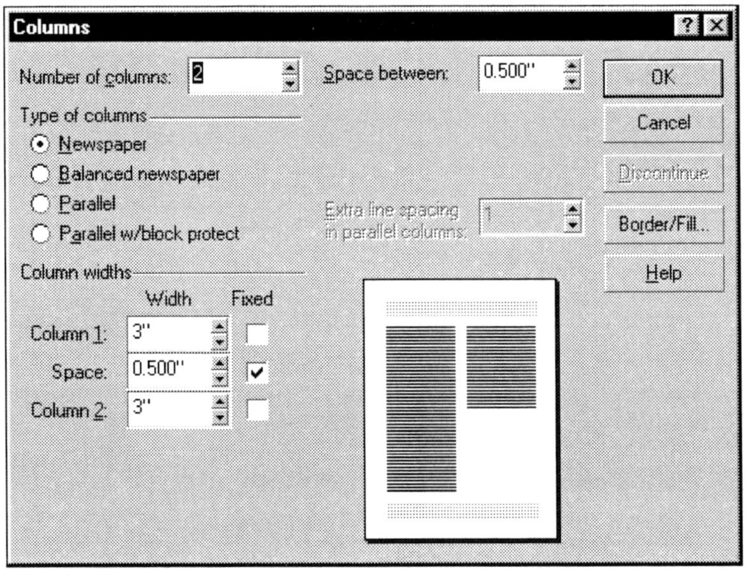

Type: **3** in the Number of columns text box

Click: **Balanced newspaper** in the Type of columns section

Click: the **OK** button

The text is displayed in a three-column format with the text equally balanced in each column.

NOTE: Column guidelines are displayed surrounding each of the three columns.

3. Change the view display to full page view.

Click: the **Zoom** button 

Click: **Full Page**

The document is displayed in full page view and should look similar to the following:

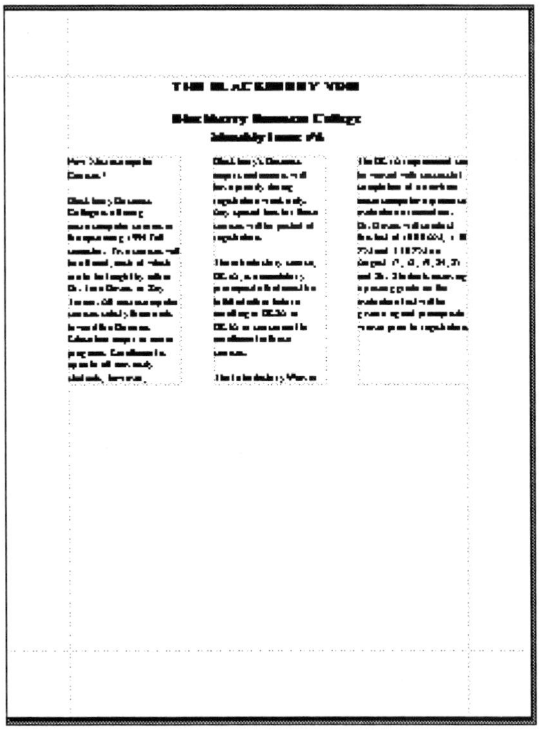

4. Change the number of columns.

Click: **Format** on the menu bar

Click: **Columns** on the Format menu

The Columns dialog box is displayed.

Type: **2**

Click: the **OK** button

The text is displayed in a two-column format and should look similar to the following:

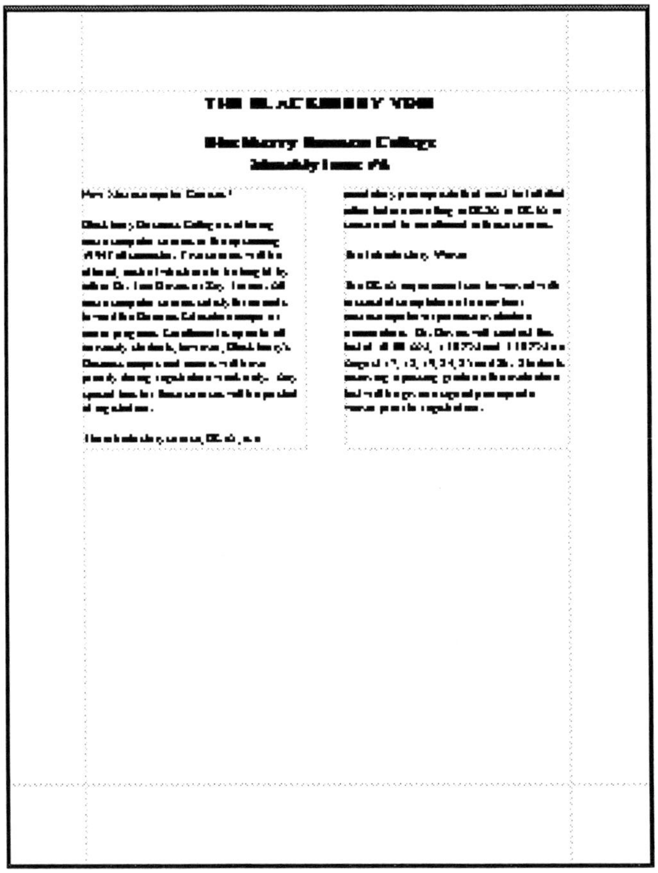

Click: the **Zoom** button 

Click: **Margin Width**

The document is displayed in margin width view.

5. **Move around between columns using the keyboard.**

Press: **[Alt] + [End]**

The insertion point is positioned in the last line of the current column.

Press: **[Alt] + [Right Arrow]**

The insertion point is positioned at the bottom of the second column.

Press: **[Alt] + [Left Arrow]**

The insertion point is positioned in the first column.

Press: **[Alt] + [Home]**

The insertion point is positioned at the top of the current column.

6. **On your own, save the current version of the document.**

Modifying the Column Format

For Your Information

Once you have defined a column format, you can modify the format by adjusting the space between columns and the width and spacing within a column.

Changing Column Width and Spacing

You modify the width of columns and the spacing between columns, often called the gutter, using the Columns command on the Format menu.

To modify column width and spacing:

- Click Format on the menu bar.
- Click Columns on the Format menu to display the following:

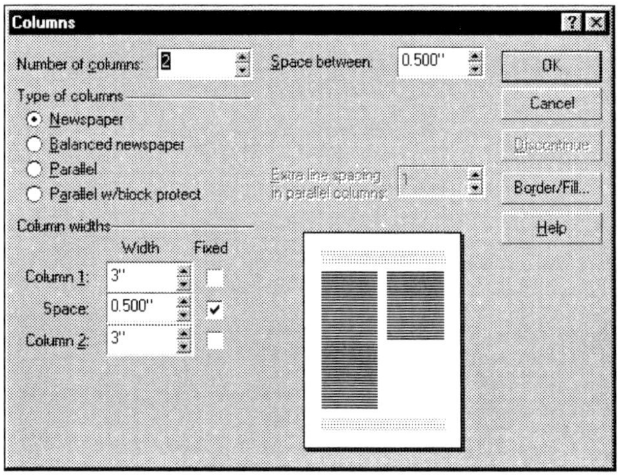

- Type a new number in the Space between text box.
- In the Column widths section, type a number in the appropriate column text box.
- In the Column widths section, type a number in the Space text box to change column spacing between specific columns.
- Click the OK button.

Modifying Columns Using Guidelines and the Ruler Bar

Guidelines show the column margins and gutter width. The guidelines display onscreen, but do not print. You can quickly adjust a column margin or gutter width by simply dragging the desired guideline, as displayed below:

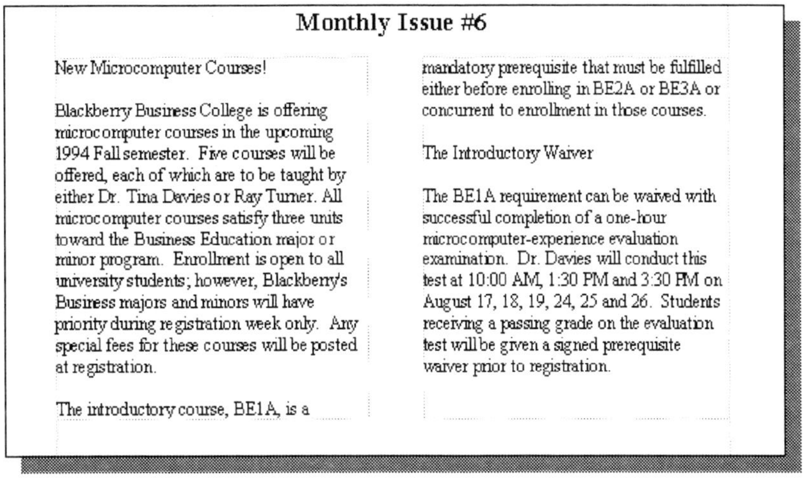
Monthly Issue #6

New Microcomputer Courses!

Blackberry Business College is offering microcomputer courses in the upcoming 1994 Fall semester. Five courses will be offered, each of which are to be taught by either Dr. Tina Davies or Ray Turner. All microcomputer courses satisfy three units toward the Business Education major or minor program. Enrollment is open to all university students; however, Blackberry's Business majors and minors will have priority during registration week only. Any special fees for these courses will be posted at registration.

The introductory course, BE1A, is a mandatory prerequisite that must be fulfilled either before enrolling in BE2A or BE3A or concurrent to enrollment in those courses.

The Introductory Waiver

The BE1A requirement can be waived with successful completion of a one-hour microcomputer-experience evaluation examination. Dr. Davies will conduct this test at 10:00 AM, 1:30 PM and 3:30 PM on August 17, 18, 19, 24, 25 and 26. Students receiving a passing grade on the evaluation test will be given a signed prerequisite waiver prior to registration.

You can use the ruler bar to adjust column margins by positioning the insertion point on the column width or column margin marker and dragging the marker to the new position, as displayed below:

TRY IT 3-2 — Customizing the Column Format

In this exercise, you will change the margins and gutter width of the existing columns.

1. Using the guidelines, modify the column margins.

First: Position the insertion point on the right guideline of the first column.

Then: Drag the guideline to the left until it displays 2.75" and 0.75".

The right margin of the first column is adjusted.

Next: Position the insertion point on the left margin of the first column.

Then: Drag the guideline to the right until it displays 2.5".

The left margin of the first column is adjusted, as displayed below:

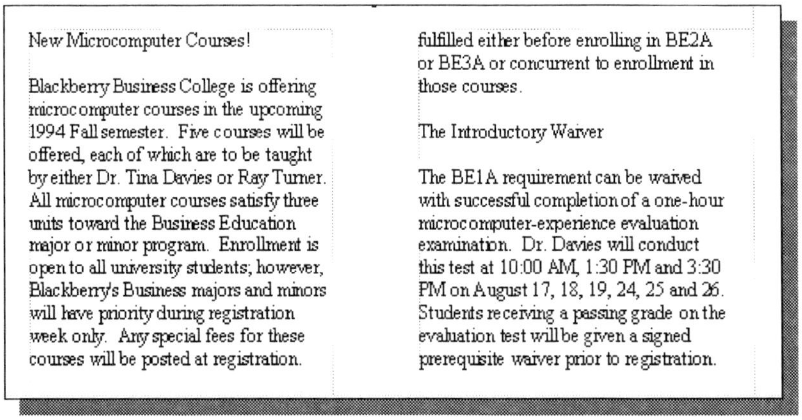
New Microcomputer Courses!

Blackberry Business College is offering microcomputer courses in the upcoming 1994 Fall semester. Five courses will be offered, each of which are to be taught by either Dr. Tina Davies or Ray Turner. All microcomputer courses satisfy three units toward the Business Education major or minor program. Enrollment is open to all university students; however, Blackberry's Business majors and minors will have priority during registration week only. Any special fees for these courses will be posted at registration.

fulfilled either before enrolling in BE2A or BE3A or concurrent to enrollment in those courses.

The Introductory Waiver

The BE1A requirement can be waived with successful completion of a one-hour microcomputer-experience evaluation examination. Dr. Davies will conduct this test at 10:00 AM, 1:30 PM and 3:30 PM on August 17, 18, 19, 24, 25 and 26. Students receiving a passing grade on the evaluation test will be given a signed prerequisite waiver prior to registration.

2. **On your own, display the ruler bar, if necessary.**

3. **Modify the right margin of the second column.**

First:	Position the insertion point on the right margin marker of the second column.
Next:	Drag the marker to the left to the 7.25" mark on the ruler.

The margin is adjusted.

4. **Adjust the spacing between columns.**

First:	Make sure the insertion point is positioned in one of the columns.
Click:	**Format** on the menu bar
Click:	**Columns** on the Format menu

The Columns dialog box is displayed.

Next:	Double-click in the **Space between** text box.

The current setting is selected.

Type:	**.35**
Click:	the **OK** button

The gutter width is adjusted, and the columns are redisplayed as balanced, similar to the following:

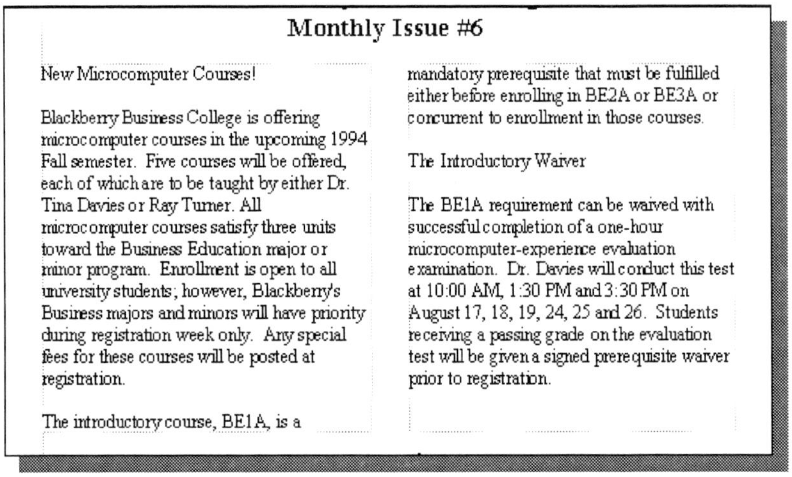
Monthly Issue #6

New Microcomputer Courses!

Blackberry Business College is offering microcomputer courses in the upcoming 1994 Fall semester. Five courses will be offered, each of which are to be taught by either Dr. Tina Davies or Ray Turner. All microcomputer courses satisfy three units toward the Business Education major or minor program. Enrollment is open to all university students; however, Blackberry's Business majors and minors will have priority during registration week only. Any special fees for these courses will be posted at registration.

The introductory course, BE1A, is a mandatory prerequisite that must be fulfilled either before enrolling in BE2A or BE3A or concurrent to enrollment in those courses.

The Introductory Waiver

The BE1A requirement can be waived with successful completion of a one-hour microcomputer-experience evaluation examination. Dr. Davies will conduct this test at 10:00 AM, 1:30 PM and 3:30 PM on August 17, 18, 19, 24, 25 and 26. Students receiving a passing grade on the evaluation test will be given a signed prerequisite waiver prior to registration.

5. Print the current version of the document.

Click: the **Print** button on the toolbar

The Print dialog box is displayed.

Click: the **Print** button

The document is printed.

6. On your own, save and close the document window.

Creating a Table

For Your Information

Using the Table command on the Insert menu or the Table QuickCreate button on the toolbar, you can set up tables of varying dimensions. These tables can include text, numbers, and formulas.

Inserting a Table

A *table* is made up of vertical columns and horizontal rows that intersect to form cells. Each cell is identified by an address; for example, A1 is the address for column A, row 1; B3 is the address for column B, row 3. The number of columns and rows can be easily defined through the Create Table dialog box, as shown below:

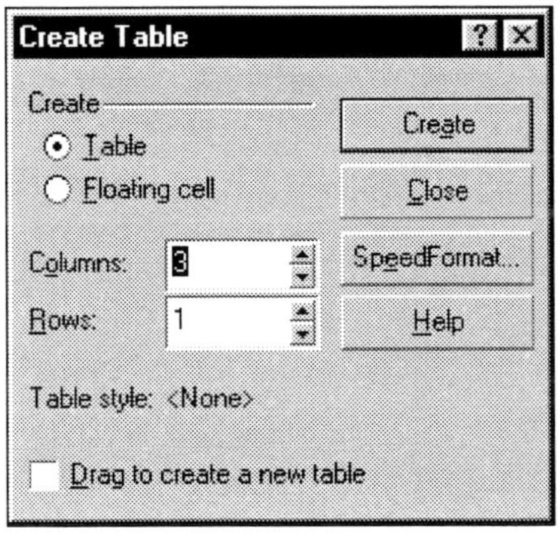

Entering Data in a Table

To enter data in a table, you position the insertion point in the appropriate cell and begin typing. Text wraps within a cell as it does within the margins of a document. When the insertion point reaches the right boundary of a cell, it automatically moves to the next line, expanding the height of that row by one line. Pressing [Enter] also moves the insertion point to the next line and increases the row height.

Moving the Insertion Point and Selecting Cells

The methods for moving the insertion point and selecting text in a table are similar to those used in other parts of a document. The standard arrow keys move the insertion point within a cell; [Tab] and [Shift] + [Tab] move the insertion point to the next and previous cells, respectively.

To select rows, columns, and specific cells, you position the insertion point in the table, next to the top or left border of a cell. The insertion point will display as a small pointer arrow. You then click the left mouse button to select the column or row to which you are pointing. You can also select cells by dragging the mouse pointer over the columns and rows.

Adjusting Column Width

You adjust column width in a table by positioning the insertion point on any cell border. When the insertion point becomes a vertical bar with side arrows, you drag the cell border to adjust the column width and resize the overall table. You can also adjust the table column width by displaying the ruler bar, then dragging the column margin markers.

TRY IT 3–3 — Creating a Table

In this exercise, you will create a table, then enter information into the table.

1. Create a three-column by five-row table.

Click: **Insert** on the menu bar

Click: **Table** on the Insert menu

TIP
You can also press [F12] to display the Create Table dialog box.

The Create Table dialog box is displayed, as follows:

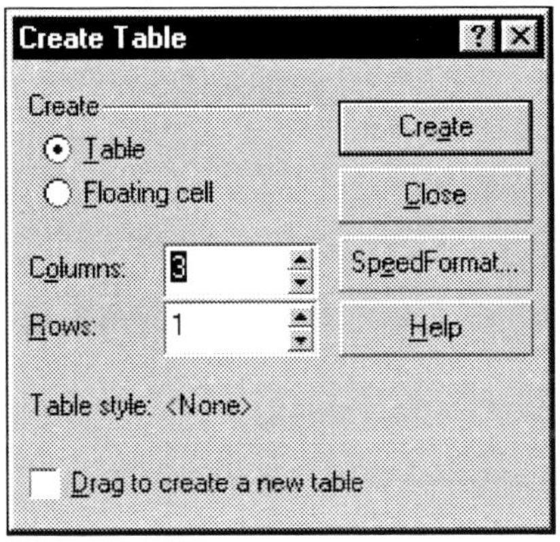

Type: **3** in the Columns text box, if necessary

Press: **[Tab]**

Type: **5** in the Rows text box

Click: the **Create** button

The table is created.

2. **Enter the first row of data.**

First: Make sure the insertion point is located in cell A1.

NOTE: The current cell address is displayed on the status bar.

Type: **Expenses**

Press: **[Tab]**

The text is inserted into cell A1 and the insertion point is displayed in cell B1.

Type: **Cost per quarter**

Press: **[Tab]**

The text is inserted into cell B1 and the insertion point is displayed in cell C1.

Type: **Cost per year**

Press: **[Tab]**

The text is inserted into cell C1 and the insertion point is displayed in cell A2.

3. **Enter the second row of table information.**

Type: **Tuition**

Press: **[Tab]**

Type: **950.00**

Press: **[Tab] [Tab]**

No text is inserted in cell C2, and the second row of data is entered.

4. On your own, enter the remaining data, as displayed below:

Expenses	Cost per quarter	Cost per year
Tuition	950.00	
Books	100.00	
Supplies	150.00	
Total		

5. Adjust the table column width.

First: Position the insertion point on the left border of the first column.

NOTE: The insertion point displays as a double arrow when properly positioned.

Then: Drag the border to the right until the position number displays 1.85".

The column width is adjusted.

6. Save the table.

Click: the **Save** button 

The Save File dialog box is displayed.

Type: **Expenses**

Click: the **Save** button

The table is saved.

Modifying the Appearance of a Table

For Your Information

Once a table is created, you can modify its appearance by inserting and deleting columns and rows, merging cells within the table, and bolding and centering text within the table. You can also change the numeric format of data.

Inserting and Deleting Columns and Rows

After creating a table, you may need to increase or decrease the table size. This can be done by inserting or deleting, respectively, one or more columns/rows.

To insert columns/rows:

- Right-click at the position you wish to insert a column or row.

- Click Insert on the object menu to display the following:

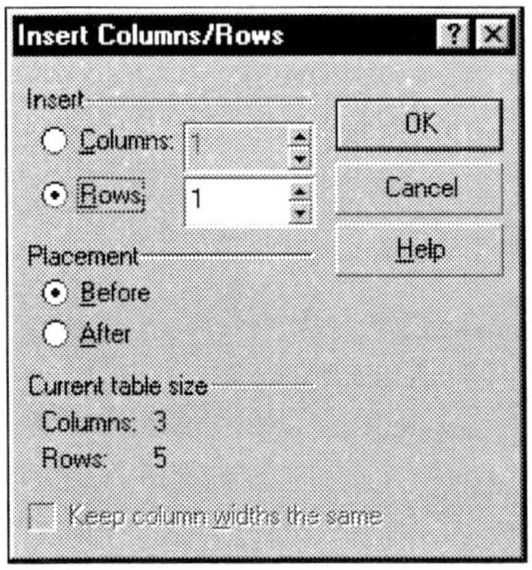

- In the Insert section, click Columns or Rows, then type the number of columns or rows you wish to insert in the respective text box.

- In the Placement section, select Before to insert the column or row before the current insertion point location or After to insert the column or row after the current insertion point location.

- Click the OK button.

Joining Cells

You can combine two or more cells to create one cell for entering special information, such as a title or other heading. If cells are already joined, you can split the cells to form additional cells. These tasks are accomplished with the Join and Split commands on the Table menu.

Formatting Table Text

To format the text in a table, you begin by selecting the desired text or cell containing the text, then clicking the appropriate button on the toolbar or property bar. If you select an entire row or column, all the text within the row or column will be affected, similar to the following:

Yearly Expenses		
Expenses	**Cost per quarter**	**Cost per year**
Tuition	950.00	
Books	100.00	
Supplies	150.00	
Total		

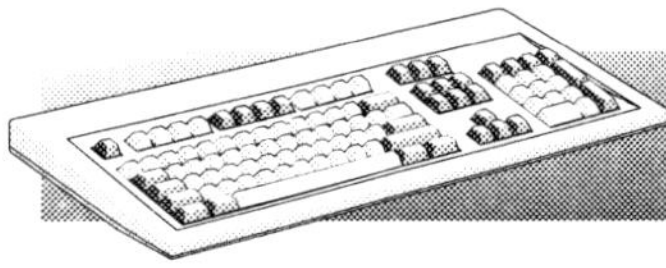

TRY IT 3-4 — Modifying a Table

In this exercise, you will modify the structure of the current table by adjusting the column width, inserting a row of cells, and joining two cells. You will also format text in the table.

1. Insert a row in the table.

First: Right-click cell A1.

An object menu is displayed.

Click: **Insert** on the object menu

The Insert Columns/Rows dialog box is displayed, as follows:

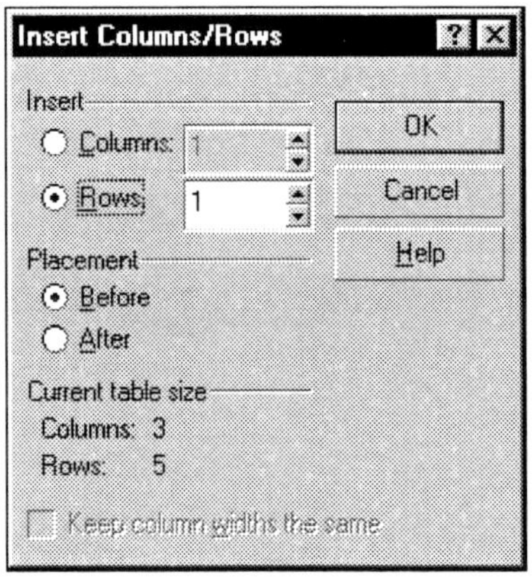

NOTE: Because of the insertion point location, the Before option in the Placement section is selected by default.

Click: the **OK** button

A row is inserted above the insertion point location, and the insertion point is positioned in the new cell A1.

2. **Enter a bold heading in the new row.**

Type: **Yearly Expenses**

The heading is entered.

Next: Select cell A1.

Click: the **Bold** button on the toolbar

Press: **[Home]**

The title is bolded and the cell is deselected.

3. **Join the cells in row one, then center the text.**

First: Select row one by pointing the arrow toward the left column margin, and double-clicking.

Next: Right-click the selected row.

Click: **Join Cells** on the object menu

The cells in row one are joined into a single cell.

Click: the **Justification** button on the property bar

The Justification drop-down list is expanded.

Click: **Center**

The heading text is centered.

4. **On your own, bold and center the headings in row 2, similar to the following:**

Yearly Expenses		
Expenses	**Cost per quarter**	**Cost per year**
Tuition	950.00	
Books	100.00	
Supplies	150.00	
Total		

5. **Save, then print, the current version of the document.**

Click: the **Save** button  on the toolbar

The file is saved.

Click: the **Print** button  on the toolbar

The Print dialog box is displayed.

Click: the **Print** button

The current version of the document is printed.

Performing Table Calculations

For Your Information

Using WordPerfect's Table feature, you can perform spreadsheet operations on data in a table. Some of the spreadsheet functions you can perform include creating a formula, copying a formula, and using WordPerfect's built-in functions.

Creating a Formula

Formulas consist of two elements: values and operators. *Values* are constant numbers or cell addresses; *operators* are symbols that indicate what to do with the values.

To create a formula:

- Right-click the cell that will contain the result of the formula.
- Click Formula Toolbar on the object menu to display the following:

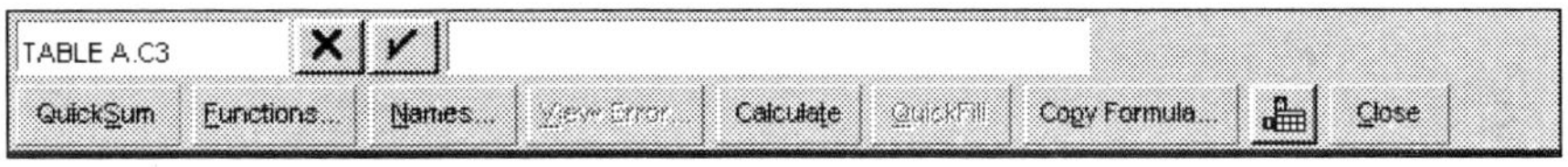

- Type the formula in the Enter or edit a formula text box.
- Click the Insert button on the formula toolbar.

Copying a Formula

Once a formula is created, you can copy it to other cells in the table. You do this by either clicking Copy Formula on the object menu, or by clicking the Copy Formula button on the formula toolbar.

To copy a formula using the formula toolbar:

- Position the insertion point in the cell you wish to copy.
- Click the Copy Formula button.
- To copy the formula to a specific cell, type the cell address in the To Cell text box.
- To copy the formula down or to the right of the current location, type the number of times to copy in the Down or Right text boxes, respectively.
- Click the OK button.

Using the Sum Function

One of WordPerfect's built-in functions is the QuickSum function. The *QuickSum* function adds up a column of values above or to the left of the insertion point. You can access the QuickSum function from the formula toolbar, or by clicking QuickSum on the object menu.

To sum a column of numbers:

- Right-click the cell that will contain the result of the sum.
- Click QuickSum on the object menu.

Changing Numeric Format

You can also change the format of values in a table using the Numeric Format dialog box. You can change values to display in a variety of formats including currency, percent, and scientific.

To change the numeric format of values in a table:

- Select the desired cells.
- Right-click the selected cells.
- Click Numeric Format on the object menu to display the following dialog box:

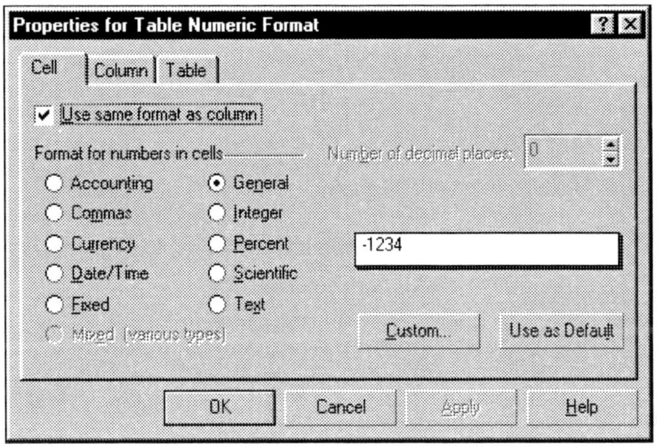

- Select the desired format.
- Click the OK button.

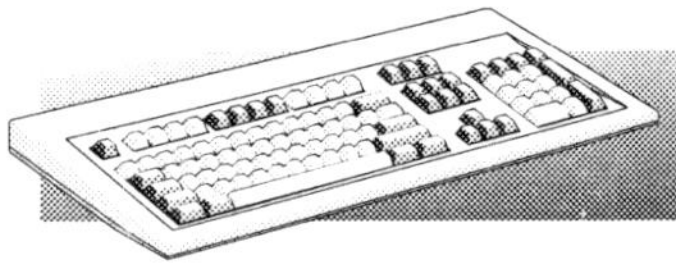

TRY IT 3-5 — Creating Table Formulas

In this exercise, you will open an expense file, then create and copy formulas to other cells.

1. Calculate the yearly tuition expense.

First: Right-click cell C3.

Click: **Formula Toolbar** on the object menu

The formula toolbar is displayed below the property bar, similar to the following:

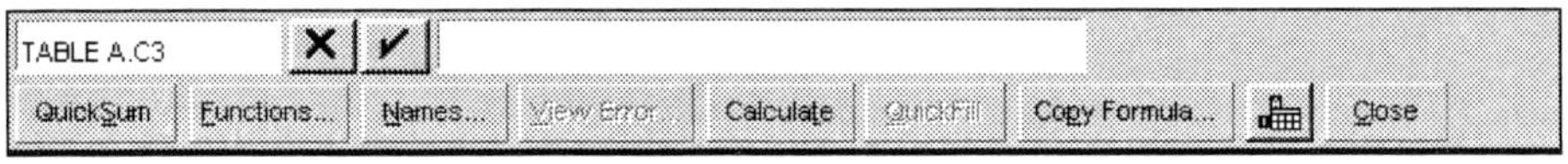

Next: Click in the **Enter or edit a formula** text box.

Formula edit mode is turned on.

Type: **b3*2**

Click: the **Insert** button  on the formula toolbar

A formula that multiplies the semester tuition by 2 is created, and the result (1900) is entered into cell C3.

2. Copy the formula down to calculate the other expenses.

Click: the **Copy Formula** button on the formula toolbar

The Copy Formula dialog box is displayed, as follows:

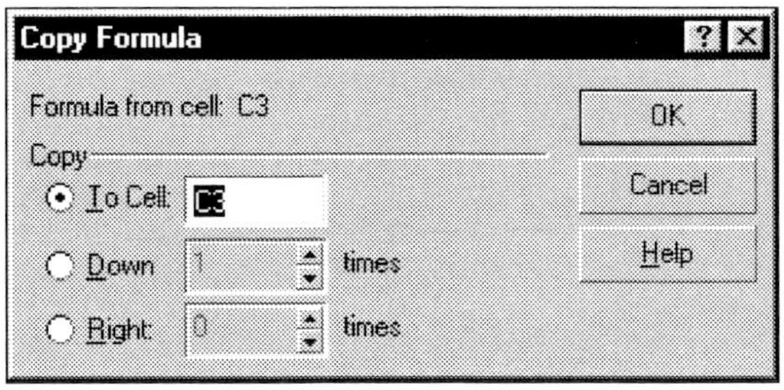

Click:	**Down** in the Copy section
Type:	**2**
Click:	the **OK** button

The formula is copied down two cells, and the results of the calculations are displayed in the cells.

3. **Sum the semester expenses to get a total in cell B6, then copy the formula to cell C5.**

First:	Position the insertion point in cell B6.
Click:	the **QuickSum** button on the formula toolbar

The total of column B (1200) is displayed in cell B6.

Click:	the **Copy Formula** button on the formula toolbar
Click:	**Right** in the Destination section
Then:	If necessary, type **1**.
Click:	the **OK** button

TIP
You can also create a QuickSum calculation by using [Ctrl]+ [=].

The sum formula is copied to the right, and the result (2400) is displayed in cell C5, similar to the following:

Yearly Expenses		
Expenses	Cost per quarter	Cost per year
Tuition	950.00	1900
Books	100.00	200
Supplies	150.00	300
Total	1200	2400

Click: the **Close** button on the formula toolbar

The formula toolbar is removed.

4. Format the values in the table.

First: Select cells **B3** through **C6**.

Next: Right-click the selected cells

Click: **Numeric Format** on the object menu

The Numeric Format dialog box is displayed.

Click: the **Table** tab

Table options are displayed, as follows:

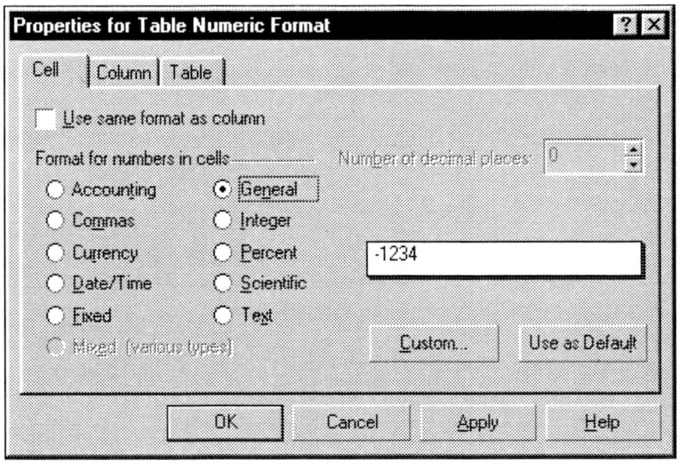

Click: **Currency**

The format is selected.

Click: the **OK** button

The format is applied to the selected cells.

Press: **[Home]**

The cells are deselected, and the table should look similar to the following:

Yearly Expenses		
Expenses	**Cost per quarter**	**Cost per year**
Tuition	$950.00	$1,900.00
Books	$100.00	$200.00
Supplies	$150.00	$300.00
Total	$1,200.00	$2,400.00

5. **On your own, save the current version of the file, then close the document window.**

Summary of Lesson 3

To define columns:

- Position the insertion point where you want the columns to begin.
- Click **Format** on the menu bar.
- Click **Columns** on the Format menu to display the Columns dialog box.
- Type the number of columns desired in the Number of columns text box.
- Select the type of column in the Type of columns section.
- Click the **OK** button.

To modify column width and spacing:

- Click **Format** on the menu bar.
- Click **Columns** on the Format menu.
- Type a new number in the Spacing between columns text box.
- In the Column widths section, type a number in the appropriate column text box.
- In the Column widths section, type a number in the Space text box to change column spacing between specific columns.
- Click the **OK** button.

To insert columns/rows:

- Right-click at the position you wish to insert a column or row.
- Click **Insert** on the object menu.
- In the Insert section, click **Columns or Rows**, then type the number of columns or rows you wish to insert in the respective text box.
- In the Placement section, select **Before** to insert the column or row before the current insertion point location, or **After** to insert the column or row after the current insertion point location.
- Click the **OK** button.

To create a formula:

- Right-click the cell that will contain the result of the formula.
- Click **Formula Toolbar** on the object menu.
- Type the formula in the Edit Formula text box.
- Click the **Insert** button on the formula toolbar.

To copy a formula using the formula toolbar:

- Right-click the cell you wish to copy.
- Click the **Copy Formula** button.
- To copy the formula to a specific cell, type the cell address in the To Cell text box in the Destination section.
- To copy the formula down or to the right of the current location, type the number of times to copy in the Down or Right text boxes, respectively.
- Click the **OK** button.

To change the numeric format of values in a table:

- Select the desired cells.
- Right-click the selected cells
- Click **Numeric Format** on the object menu.
- Select the desired format.
- Click the **OK** button.

Practice Exercise — Lesson 3

1. Open the file named Work2-3.

2. Type the following heading, followed by two blank lines:

ON-THE-GO TOURS NEWSLETTER

3. Bold and center the heading.

4. Define a two-column balanced newspaper format beginning with the text, "Are you feeling." The document should look similar to the following:

> ON-THE-GO TOURS NEWSLETTER
>
> Are you feeling a bit "stressed out" these days? On-the-Go Tours has the perfect remedy -- Hawaii! Only a 5-hour plane ride from the West Coast, the Hawaiian islands are indeed paradise. If you like the excitement of a major city, mixed with a certain laid-back attitude, you will love the glamour of Honolulu and Waikiki Beach. If you just want to get away from it all, the many resorts on Maui, Kauaii or the big island of Hawaii will surely appeal to you. Whatever you want, it is there. What's more -- On-the-Go Tours makes it <u>very</u> affordable. Just give us a call at (800) 123-4567, and then get ready to have a truly memorable experience!

5. Move to the end of the document, then turn columns off. (Hint: Click Format, Columns, Discontinue.)

6. Create a 2-column by 3-row table.

7. Type the following data in the table:

A1:	**ON-THE-GO TRAVEL**		
B1:	**3-DAY**	**B2:**	**500**
C1:	**3-MONTH**	**C2:**	**30,000**

8. Join the cells in row one, then center all the text in the table.

9. Print the file, then save it as OTGNEWS.WPD.

Lesson 4 Customizing Text and Graphics

Lesson Objectives

By the end of this lesson, you will be able to enhance documents with borders, shading, special characters, and drop caps. You will also be able to insert a header and a footer in a document, resize a document to make it fit page limitations, and customize graphic images.

You will learn how to:

- add borders and shading
- insert characters and drop caps
- add headers and footers to a document
- use the Make It Fit feature

Adding Borders and Shading

For Your Information

Borders, shading, and fill patterns are elements that can enhance the appearance of the documents you create. WordPerfect provides a variety of default borders for you to choose from and allows you to add shading and patterns to selected text in a document. Once you have selected a border style, you can also customize the border to better fit your needs.

Applying Borders and Shading

You can apply a border to a paragraph, page, or column of text. You can also fill the border with patterns or shading.

To apply a border and/or shading to a paragraph:

- Select the text to be formatted.
- Click Format on the menu bar.
- Select Paragraph on the Format menu.
- Click Border/Fill on the Paragraph submenu.
- In the Available border styles section, select the desired border style.
- Click the Fill tab, then in the Available fill styles section, select the desired shading or fill pattern.
- Click the OK button.

Customizing Borders

Once you have chosen a border style, you can customize the border by modifying the line style and drop shadow. For example you can customize a border style to include double lines, or change the location of a shadow border. You modify borders and shading from the respective Border/Fill dialog box.

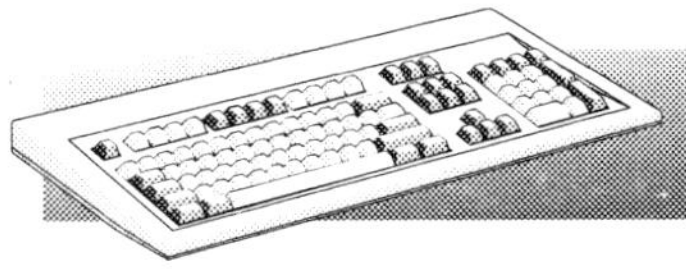

TRY IT 4–1 — Adding Borders and Shading

In this exercise, you will add borders and fill patterns to text in a newsletter.

1. On your own, open the file named Compnws.

2. Place a drop shadow border around the centered title at the top of the document.

First:	Select the three centered lines at the top of the document.
Click:	**Format** on the menu bar
Select:	**Paragraph** on the Format menu
Click:	**Border/Fill** on the Paragraph submenu

TIP
To add a single horizontal line border, press the Hyphen key 4 times, then press [Enter].

The Paragraph Border/Fill dialog box is displayed, as follows:

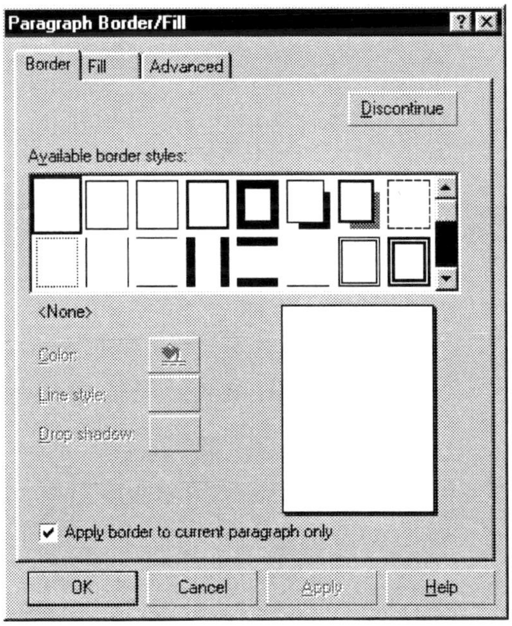

Next: In the Available border styles section, select the sixth border button in the first row (Shadow).

A shadow border is displayed in the preview section.

Click: the **OK** button

A drop shadow border is inserted around the centered text.

Press: **[Home]**

The text is deselected and should look similar to the following:

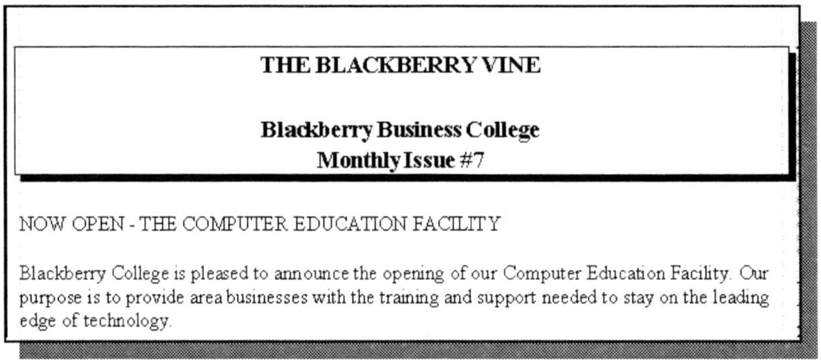
THE BLACKBERRY VINE

Blackberry Business College
Monthly Issue #7

NOW OPEN - THE COMPUTER EDUCATION FACILITY

Blackberry College is pleased to announce the opening of our Computer Education Facility. Our purpose is to provide area businesses with the training and support needed to stay on the leading edge of technology.

TIP
To add a double horizontal line border, press the [=] key 4 times, then press [Enter].

3. Place a customized, two-line border around a subheading.

First: Select the subheading beginning, “NOW OPEN.”

Click: **Format** on the menu bar

Select: **Paragraph** on the Format menu

Click: **Border/Fill** on the Paragraph submenu

Next: Click the third border style in the second row (Thin Top/Bottom).

The border style is selected.

Next: Click the Line style button and select the second style in the top row (Double).

The customized border is displayed in the preview section.

Click: the **OK** button

A customized, two-line border is displayed around the text.

Press: **[Home]**

The text is deselected, and the document should look similar to the following:

THE BLACKBERRY VINE

Blackberry Business College
Monthly Issue #7

NOW OPEN - THE COMPUTER EDUCATION FACILITY

4. Shade text in the document.

First: Select the title, "Customized Programs."

Click: **Format** on the menu bar

Select: **Paragraph** on the Format menu

Click: **Border/Fill** on the Paragraph submenu

Next: Click the **Fill** tab.

Fill options are displayed, similar to the following:

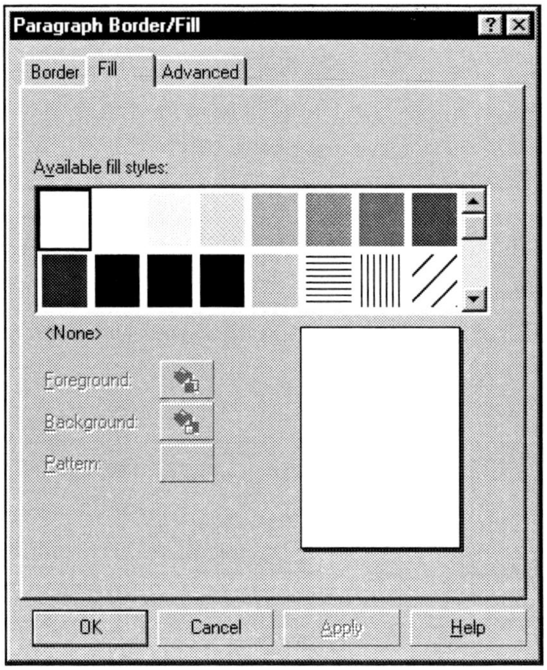

Then: Select the fifth fill option in the second row (Button Fill).

The fill option is selected.

Click: the **OK** button

The text is displayed shaded in the document window.

Press: **[Home]**

The text is deselected and should look similar to the following:

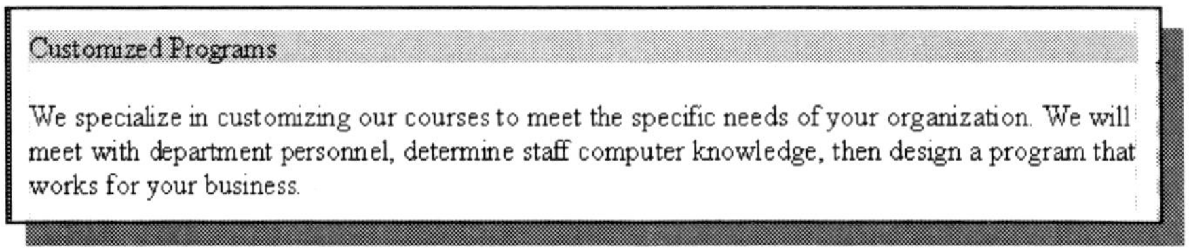

5. On your own, save the current version of the document.

Inserting Characters and Drop Caps

For Your Information

You can further enhance the appearance of your documents by adding special characters and drop caps. WordPerfect provides over 1,500 characters and symbols and many predefined drop-cap styles to help give your paragraphs a professional look.

Inserting WordPerfect Characters

WordPerfect characters are grouped into sets by type of character. You insert characters into a document by clicking Symbol on the Insert menu.

To insert a WordPerfect character:

- Position the insertion point at the desired location.
- Click Insert on the menu bar.
- Click Symbol on the Insert menu to display the following:

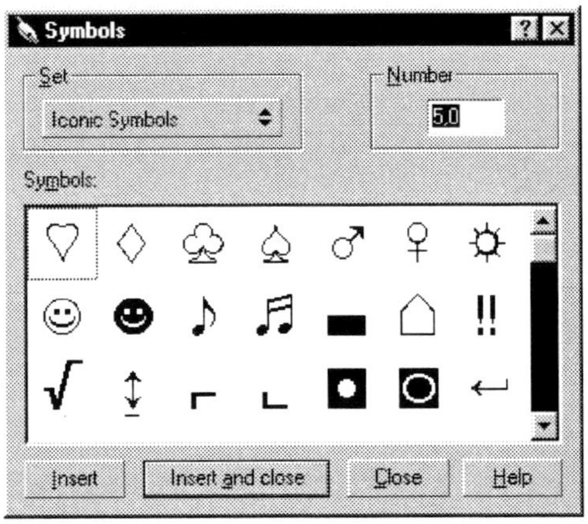

- Expand the Set list box and choose a character set.
- Click the character you want to insert in the Symbols list box.
- Click the Insert button to insert the character and leave the dialog box open, or click the Insert and close button to insert the character and close the dialog box.

Inserting Drop Caps

You use the Drop Cap command on the Format, Paragraph submenu to enlarge the first character or word of a paragraph, as displayed below:

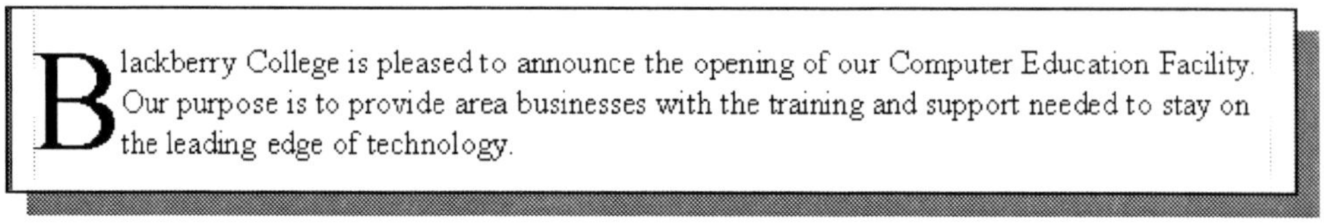
Blackberry College is pleased to announce the opening of our Computer Education Facility. Our purpose is to provide area businesses with the training and support needed to stay on the leading edge of technology.

When you insert a drop cap, the Drop Cap property bar is automatically displayed below the toolbar bar. The property bar contains buttons that allow you to customize the appearance of drop caps, as displayed below:

Drop Cap Style expands the Drop Cap palette and allows you to select a predefined drop cap style.

Drop Cap Size allows you to select the line height of the drop cap.

Drop Cap Position displays a dialog box you can use to set the position of the drop cap relative to the margin.

Drop Cap Font displays options for the drop cap font.

Drop Cap Border/Fill displays options for a border and fill for the drop cap.

Drop Cap Options displays customization options for the drop cap.

To add a drop cap to a paragraph:

- Position the insertion point in the desired paragraph.
- Click Format on the menu bar.
- Select Paragraph on the Format menu.
- Click Drop Cap on the Paragraph submenu.

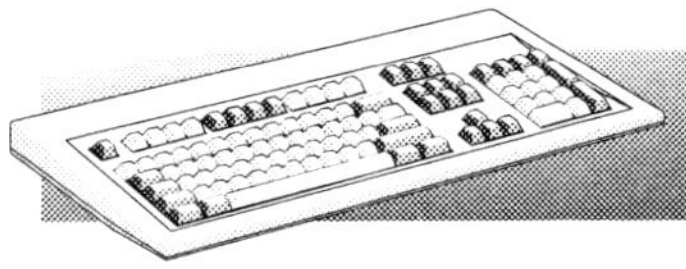

TRY IT 4–2 — Inserting Characters and Drop Caps

In this exercise, you will insert characters and a drop cap in the current document.

NOTE: Depending on the font you are using, some characters may not display onscreen and will instead display as a hollow box. They may, however, still print, depending on the graphics your printer supports.

1. Add a bulleted list of text.

First: Position the insertion point in the blank line above "Customized Programs."

Press: **[Tab] [Tab]**

Click: **Insert** on the menu bar

Click: **Symbol** on the Insert menu

The Symbols dialog box is displayed, as follows:

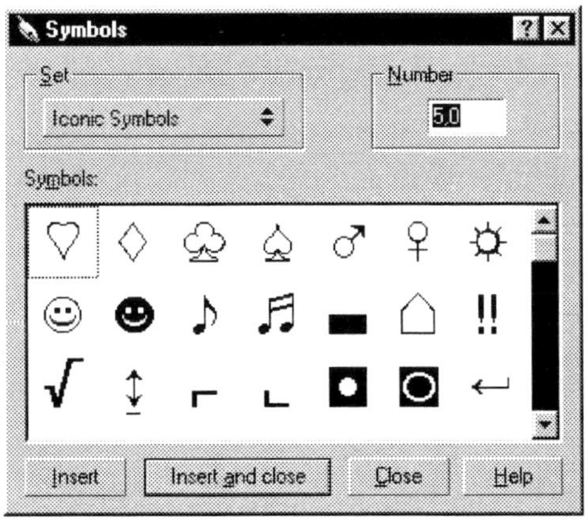

Click: the **checkmark symbol (5,14)** in the Symbols section

Click: the **Insert and close** button

A checkmark is inserted, and the dialog box is closed.

Press: **[Tab]**

Type: **Computer Fundamentals**

Press: **[Enter]**

The first bulleted item is entered.

2. **On your own, enter the remaining bulleted text. The document should look similar to the following:**

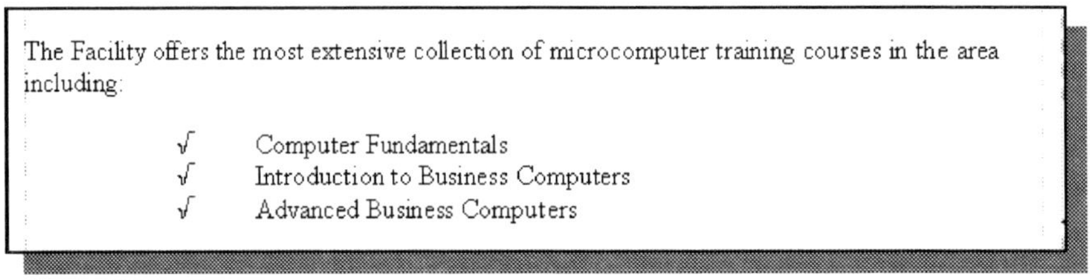
The Facility offers the most extensive collection of microcomputer training courses in the area including:

√ Computer Fundamentals
√ Introduction to Business Computers
√ Advanced Business Computers

3. **Add additional symbols to the document.**

First: Position the insertion point before the text beginning, "NOW OPEN."

Click: **Insert** on the menu bar

Click: **Symbol** on the Insert menu

Type: **5,152** in the Number text box

The character set 5, symbol number 152 (fat, right-pointing arrow) is displayed with a dotted box around it in the Symbols list box.

Click: the **Insert** button

The arrow is inserted before the title.

NOTE: The Symbols dialog box remains open.

Next: Click in the document window to activate it, then position the insertion point before the title, "Customized Programs."

Click: the **Insert and close** button

The arrow is inserted, and the Symbols dialog box is closed. The document should look similar to the following:

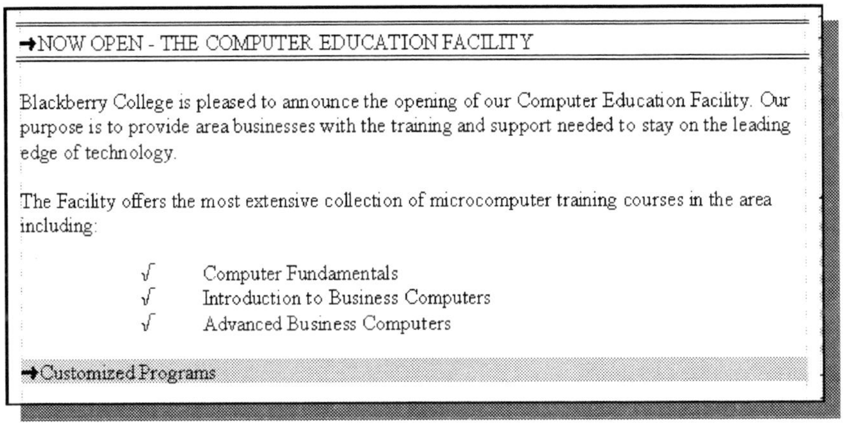
➔NOW OPEN - THE COMPUTER EDUCATION FACILITY

Blackberry College is pleased to announce the opening of our Computer Education Facility. Our purpose is to provide area businesses with the training and support needed to stay on the leading edge of technology.

The Facility offers the most extensive collection of microcomputer training courses in the area including:

√ Computer Fundamentals
√ Introduction to Business Computers
√ Advanced Business Computers

➔Customized Programs

TIP
You can also create a drop cap by pressing [Ctrl] + [Shift] + [C].

4. Insert a drop cap, then customize its appearance.

First: Click anywhere in the paragraph beginning, "Blackberry College is pleased ...."

Click: **Format** on the menu bar

Select: **Paragraph** on the Format menu

Click: **Drop Cap** on the Paragraph submenu

A drop cap is inserted at the beginning of the paragraph.

Then: Click before the drop cap character at the beginning of the sentence.

The Drop Cap property bar is displayed.

Click: the **Drop Cap Style** button

The list is expanded, and various drop cap types are displayed.

Next: Click the second button in the fourth row of the Drop Cap palette.

The drop cap type is modified.

Click: the **Drop Cap Border/Fill** button

The Drop Cap Border/Fill dialog box is displayed.

Then: Click the sixth button in the top row (Shadow).

Click: the **OK** button

The drop cap is displayed with a shadow border, and the paragraph should look similar to the following:

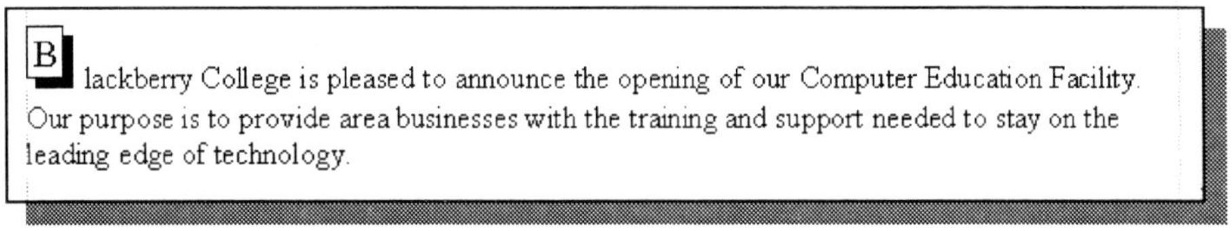
Blackberry College is pleased to announce the opening of our Computer Education Facility. Our purpose is to provide area businesses with the training and support needed to stay on the leading edge of technology.

5. **On your own, print the current version of the document, then save and close the document window.**

Adding a Header and/or Footer to a Document

For Your Information

When working with multiple-page documents, you may sometimes want certain information, such as a title, a company name, or the date, to be printed at the top or bottom of every page. Such repetitive information is called a *header* when it appears at the top of a page and a *footer* when it appears at the bottom, as displayed below:

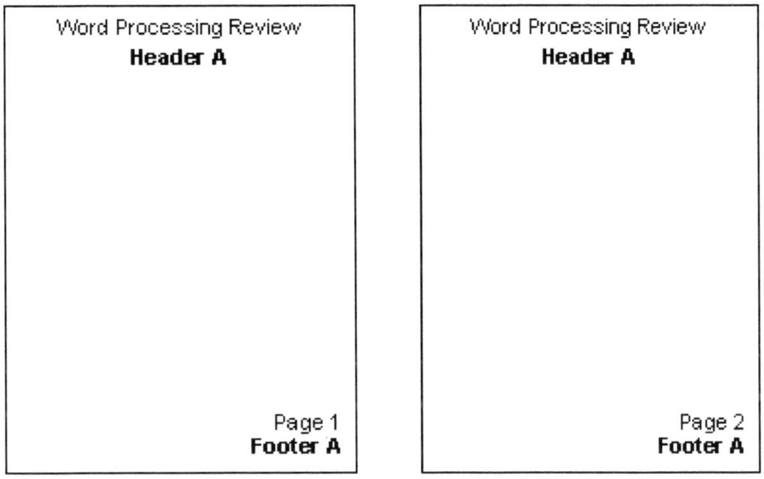

Inserting a Header or Footer

With WordPerfect, you can specify up to two headers and two footers in any document by using the Header/Footer command on the Insert menu. To add a header or footer, you position the insertion point on the page where the header/footer will begin, then display the Headers/Footers dialog box and select the desired options. You then type the header/footer text, and if desired, select the type of page number.

NOTE: Headers and footers, by default, print on every page of a document. To have them print on even or odd pages only, click the Header /Footer Placement button on the Header property bar and select a new placement.

Modifying Header/Footer Distance

When printed, headers and footers appear in the text area of the document, with the first line of a header appearing just below the top margin and the last line of a footer appearing just above the bottom margin. WordPerfect, by default, separates headers and footers from the actual text of the document by one blank line. You can increase the separation by clicking the Header/Footer Distance button on the Header property bar and typing a number in the subsequent dialog box.

Inserting the Date

WordPerfect's *Date/Time* command allows you to insert the date anywhere in a document, including headers, footers, footnotes, etc. You can insert date or time text, which will always print that date or time when the document is opened. Alternatively, you can insert a date/time code, which will display the current system date/time each time the document is opened. The date/time formats let you change the way the date displays.

To insert the date:

- Click Insert on the menu bar.
- Click Date/Time on the Insert menu to display the following:

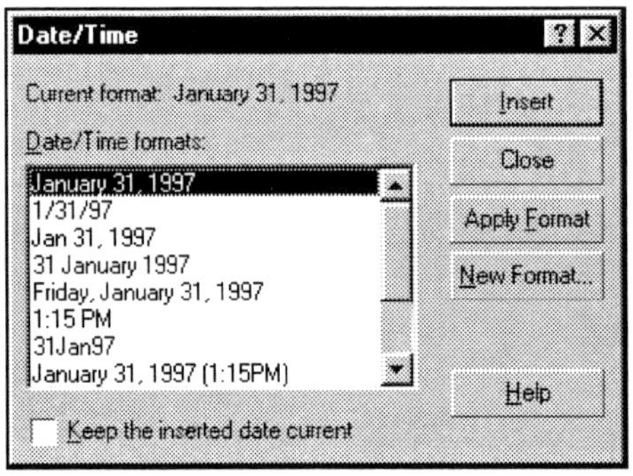

- Select the desired format.
- If the date is to be inserted as a code, click "Keep the inserted date current."
- Click the Insert button.

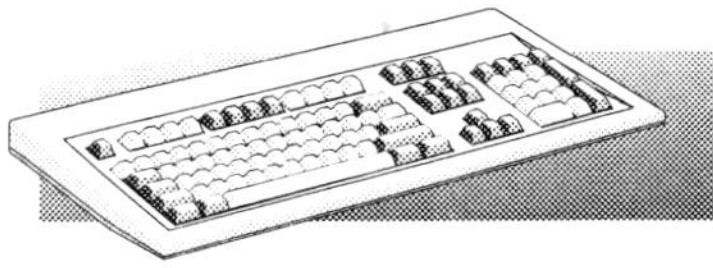

TRY IT 4–3 — Adding Headers and Footers to a Document

In this exercise, you will add a header and a footer to a document.

1. **On your own, open the file named Format2.**

2. **Begin creating a header.**

Click: **Insert** on the menu bar

Click: **Header/Footer** on the Insert menu

The Headers/Footers dialog box is displayed, as follows:

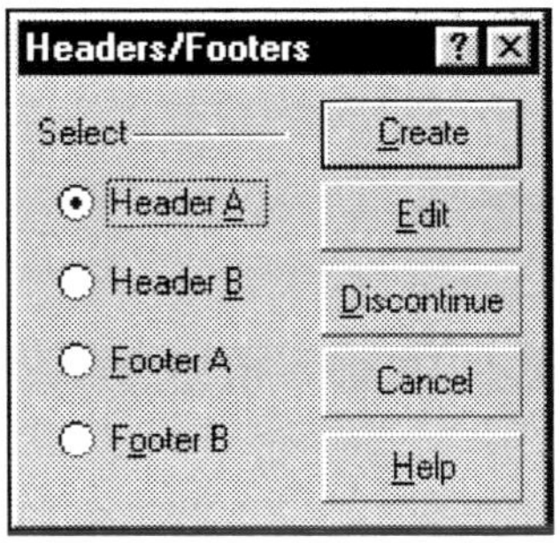

NOTE: The Header A option is selected, by default.

Click: the **Create** button

The insertion point is displayed in the header area surrounded by guidelines, and the Header/Footer property bar is displayed.

3. **Create a header with a centered title and the current date.**

First: Move the mouse pointer to the header area, and click the right mouse button.

A WordPerfect pop-up menu is displayed.

NOTE: If the insertion point is not positioned in the header area, the correct pop-up menu will not display.

Click: **Center** on the pop-up menu

Type: **WORD PROCESSING REVIEW**

Press: **[Enter]**

Next: Position the insertion point in the header area and click the right mouse button.

Click: **Center** on the pop-up menu

Click: **Insert** on the menu bar

Select: **Date/Time** on the Insert menu

Click: **Keep the inserted date curent**

Click: the **Insert** button

The current date is inserted in the header.

4. **Set the distance between the header and the beginning of the document.**

Click: the **Header/Footer Distance** button  on the Header/Footer property bar

The Distance dialog box is displayed, as follows:

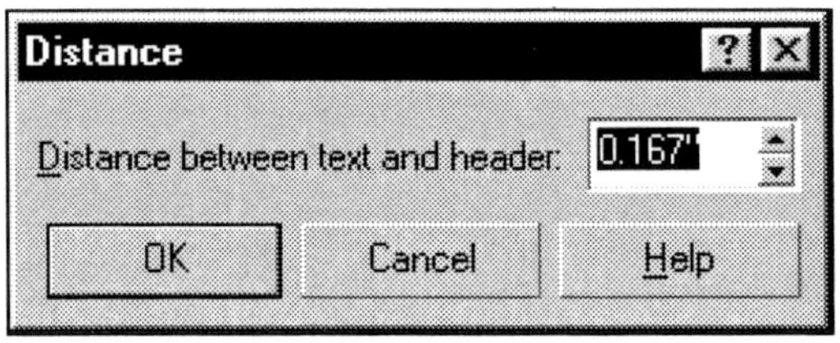

Type: **.5**

Click: the **OK** button

A half-inch space is inserted between the header and the document text, as displayed below:

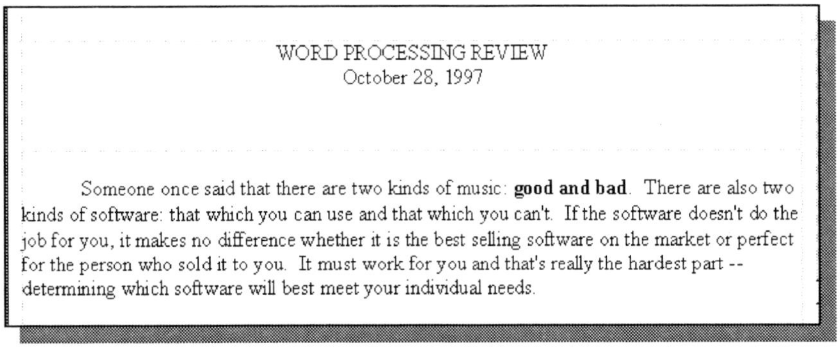
WORD PROCESSING REVIEW
October 28, 1997

Someone once said that there are two kinds of music: **good and bad**. There are also two kinds of software: that which you can use and that which you can't. If the software doesn't do the job for you, it makes no difference whether it is the best selling software on the market or perfect for the person who sold it to you. It must work for you and that's really the hardest part -- determining which software will best meet your individual needs.

Click: the **Close** button  on the Header/Footer property bar

The Header/Footer property bar is removed.

5. Begin creating a footer.

Click: **Insert** on the menu bar

Click: **Header/Footer** on the Insert menu

The Headers/Footers dialog box is displayed.

Click: **Footer A**

Click: the **Create** button

The insertion point is displayed in the footer area, and the Header/Footer property bar is turned on.

6. Enter the text of the footer.

First: Position the mouse pointer in the footer area and click the right mouse button.

Click: **Flush Right** on the pop-up menu

Type: **PAGE**

Press: **[Spacebar]**

Click: the **Page Numbering** button  on the Header/Footer property bar

A drop-down list is expanded.

Click: **Page Number**

A page number is inserted in the footer text, similar to the following:

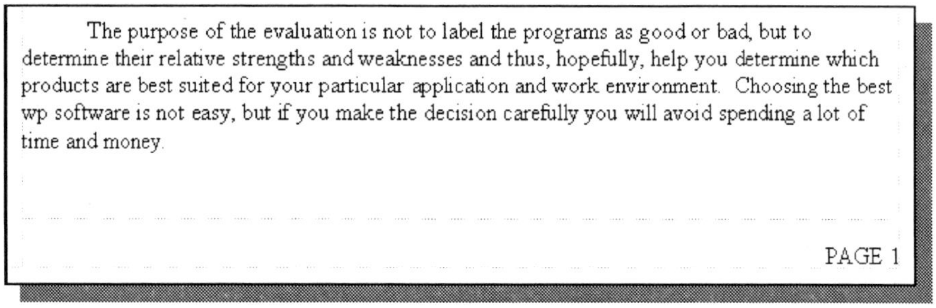

Click: the **Close** button  on the Header/Footer property bar

The Header/Footer property bar is removed.

7. Edit the footer text, and insert a horizontal line.

Click: **Insert** on the menu bar

Click: **Header/Footer** on the Insert menu

Click: **Footer A**

Click: the **Edit** button

The insertion point is displayed in the footer area.

Press: **[Enter]**

Press: **[Arrow Up]**

A blank line is inserted above the footer text. The insertion point is located on the first line.

Click: the **Horizontal Line** button 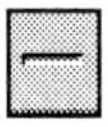 on the Header/Footer property bar

A line is inserted above the footer text, as displayed below:

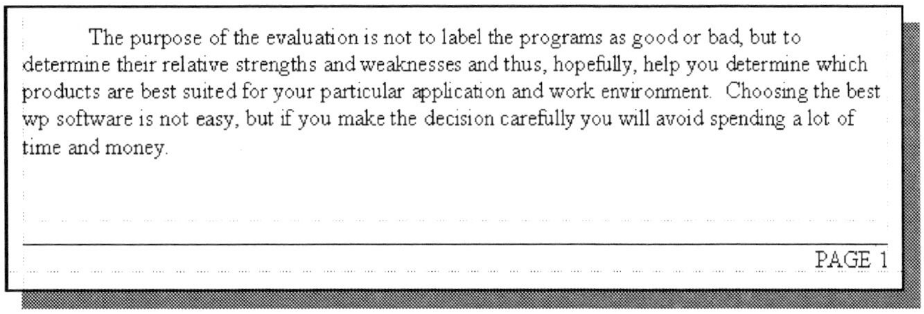
The purpose of the evaluation is not to label the programs as good or bad, but to determine their relative strengths and weaknesses and thus, hopefully, help you determine which products are best suited for your particular application and work environment. Choosing the best wp software is not easy, but if you make the decision carefully you will avoid spending a lot of time and money.

PAGE 1

Click: the **Close** button  on the Header/Footer property bar

The Header/Footer property bar is closed.

8. View the header and footer in different view modes.

First: Scroll the document window to display the header and footer text in default page mode.

Click: **View** on the menu bar

Click: **Two Pages** on the View menu

The first two pages of the document are displayed.

Click: **View** on the menu bar

Click: **Page** on the View menu

The document is returned to page view.

9. On your own, print, then save the current version of the document.

Shrinking Text to Fit on a Page

For Your Information

WordPerfect's *Make It Fit* feature shrinks or expands a document to fill a specified number of pages. For example, if you are creating a report that must fit on one page but that currently flows onto a second page, you can use the Make It Fit feature to adjust the document settings so that the entire report will fit on the first page.

Using Make It Fit

You can attempt to adjust text to fit on a single page by changing margins, font sizes, and line spacing manually, or you can let WordPerfect do it for you automatically. The Make It Fit feature will adjust text based on how many pages you want and which settings you want affected.

To use the Make It Fit feature:

- Open the desired document.
- Click Format on the menu bar.
- Click Make It Fit on the Format menu to display the following:

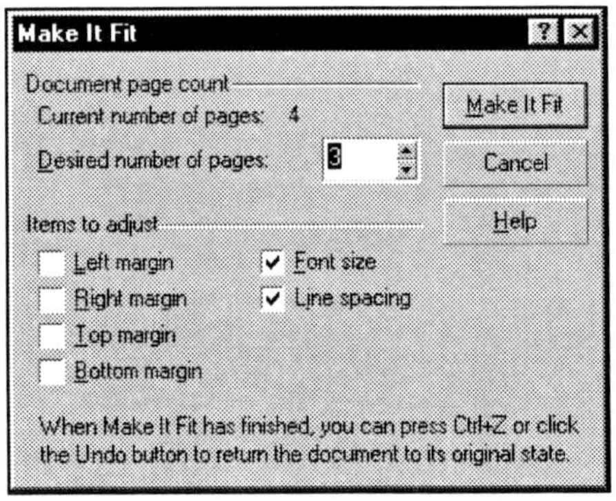

- In the Document page count section, type the desired document length in the Desired number of pages text box.
- In the Items to adjust section, select the desired options.
- Click the Make It Fit button.

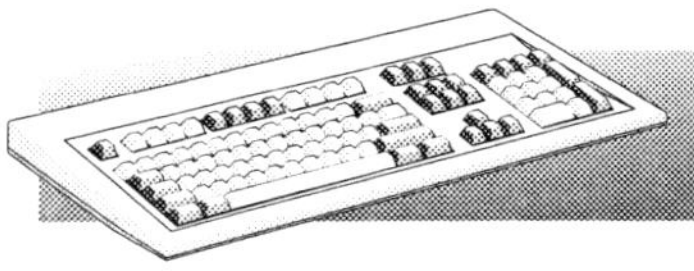

TRY IT 4-4 — Using the Make It Fit Feature

In this exercise, you will use the Make It Fit feature to shrink a four-page document onto two pages.

1. View the document in two page view.

Click: **View** on the menu bar

Click: **Two Pages** on the View menu

The document is displayed in two pages view.

Press: **[Alt]** + **[Page Down]** two times

The third page of the document is displayed in the view window.

2. Access Make It Fit and indicate the desired number of pages.

Click: **Format** on the menu bar

Click: **Make It Fit** on the Format menu

The Make It Fit dialog box is displayed, as follows:

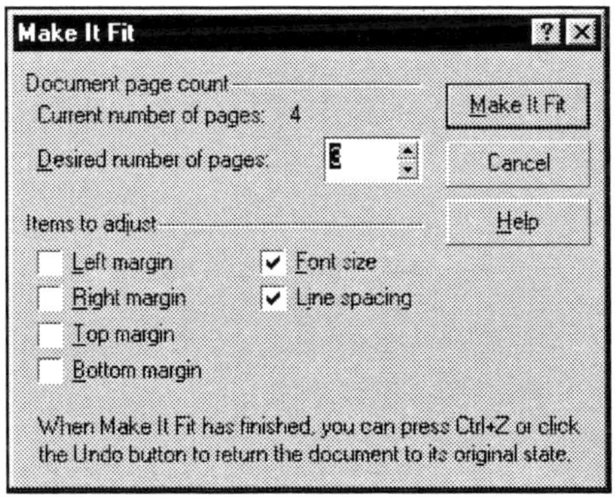

Type: **2** in the Desired number of pages text box

3. **Complete the operation.**

Click: the **Make It Fit** button

The document is adjusted to fit on two pages.

4. **View the adjustments WordPerfect made to the document's format.**

Click: **View** on the menu bar

Click: **Page** on the View menu

The document is displayed in page view.

Next: View the Font Size and Line Spacing settings on the property bar.

NOTE: You can also use reveal codes to view the new codes.

5. **On your own, close the document window without saving.**

Summary of Lesson 4

To apply a border and/or shading:

- Select the text to be formatted.
- Click **Format** on the menu bar.
- Select **Paragraph** on the Format menu.
- Click **Border/Fill** on the Paragraph submenu.
- In the Available border styles section, select the desired border style.
- Click the **Fill** tab, then in the Available fill styles section, select the desired shading or fill pattern.
- Click the **OK** button.

To insert a WordPerfect character:

- Position the insertion point at the desired location.
- Click **Insert** on the menu bar.
- Click **Symbol** on the Insert menu.
- Expand the **Set** list box and choose a character set.
- Click the character you want to insert in the Symbols list box.
- Click the **Insert** button to insert the character and leave the Symbols dialog box open, or click the **Insert and close** button to insert the character and close the dialog box.

To insert the date:

- Click **Insert** on the menu bar.
- Click **Date/Time** on the Insert menu.
- Select the desired format.
- Click the **Insert** button.

To use the Make It Fit feature:

- Open the desired document.
- Click **Format** on the menu bar.
- Click **Make It Fit** on the Format menu.
- In the Document page count section, type the desired document length in the Desired number of pages text box.
- In the Items to adjust section, select the desired options.
- Click the **Make It Fit** button.

Practice Exercise — Lesson 4

1. Open the file named Work2-4.

2. Place a shadow border around the centered, three-line title.

3. Insert character 5,113 before the titles, "NOW OPEN" and "Customized Programs."

4. Add the drop cap of your choosing to the first paragraph.

5. Add a centered footer with the current date at the bottom of the newsletter.

6. Add a single line above the date.

7. View the document in full page view, then save and print the document.

8. Close the document window.

Lesson 5 Using Merge

Lesson Objectives

By the end of this lesson, you will be able to create a data file and a form file, then merge the two files to create a document file. You will also be able to merge selected records and sort a data file.

You will learn how to:

- create a data file
- create a form file
- perform a merge
- modify the merge output
- sort a data file
- create and print an envelope

Understanding Merging

For Your Information

WordPerfect's *Merge* feature allows you to combine variable information in one document with fixed text in another to produce customized documents such as letters, invoices, and mailing labels.

Understanding the Merge Process

When merging information, WordPerfect provides a Merge dialog box that guides you through the process of creating a data file, inputting data in the file, inserting field names in the form file, and merging the two documents to create the final output.

The merge process involves the following basic steps:

- creating a data file containing the variable information that will be used to customize each form file.
- creating a form file containing the fixed text. This can be an existing document, or can be created during the merge process.
- executing the actual merge operation to combine the information in the data file and the form file.

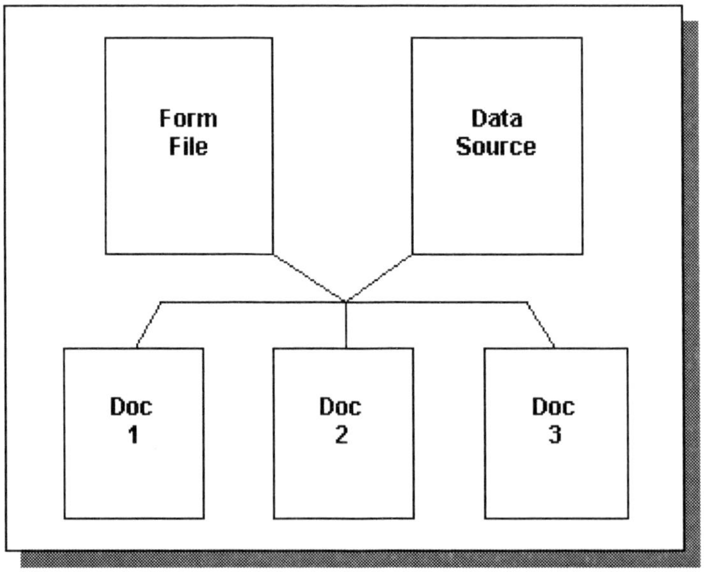

Understanding Databases

A *database* is made up of fields and records. A field contains one piece of information, while a *record* contains all of the associated fields for one database item. Similarly, in a data file, a field contains one piece of variable information, while a record contains all variable information for one document. The data file can be formatted as data text or arranged in table format. When you create a data file in text format, fields and records are separated by merge codes, and the field names appear at the top of the file:

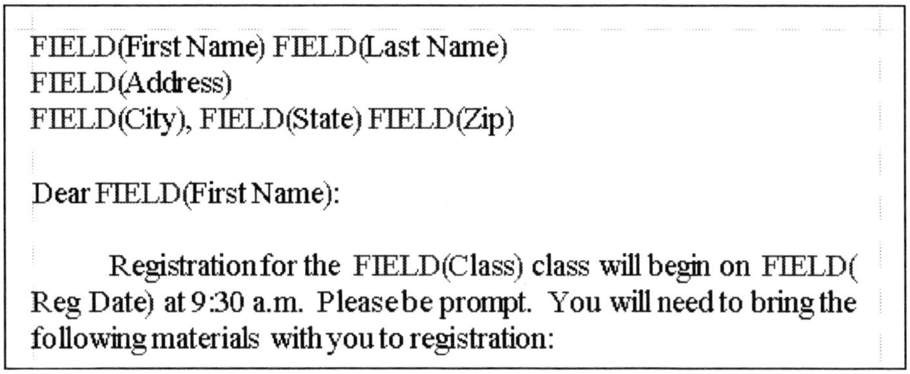
FIELD(First Name) FIELD(Last Name)
FIELD(Address)
FIELD(City), FIELD(State) FIELD(Zip)

Dear FIELD(First Name):

Registration for the FIELD(Class) class will begin on FIELD(Reg Date) at 9:30 a.m. Please be prompt. You will need to bring the following materials with you to registration:

Creating a Data File

You create a data file by first displaying the Merge dialog box. From this dialog box, you can complete most of the merge steps.

To create a data file:

- Click Tools on the menu bar.
- Click Merge on the Tools menu to display the following:

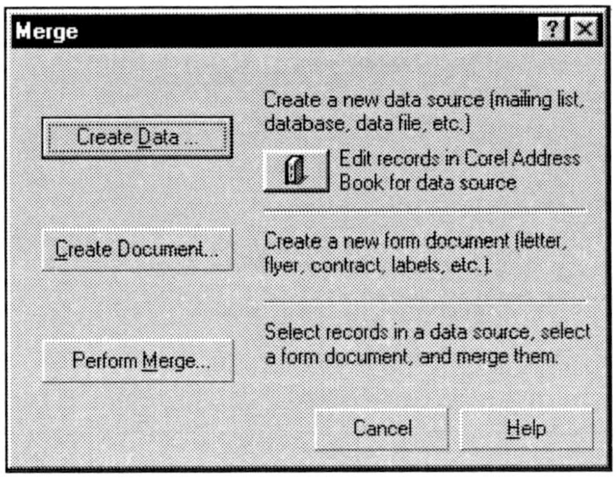

- Click the Create Data button.

NOTE: If you have a file open, WordPerfect displays the Create Merge File dialog box. If this is the case, click Use file in active window to use the open document window, or click New document window to create the data file in a new document window, then click the OK button.

- Type a field name in the Name a field text box.
- Click the Add button.
- Continue adding field names using the above steps until all the field names have been added.

Inputting Data into the Data File

Once the fields are named, the Quick Data Entry dialog box, displayed below, automatically appears. You begin entering information in the data file by typing the appropriate data in the corresponding text boxes:

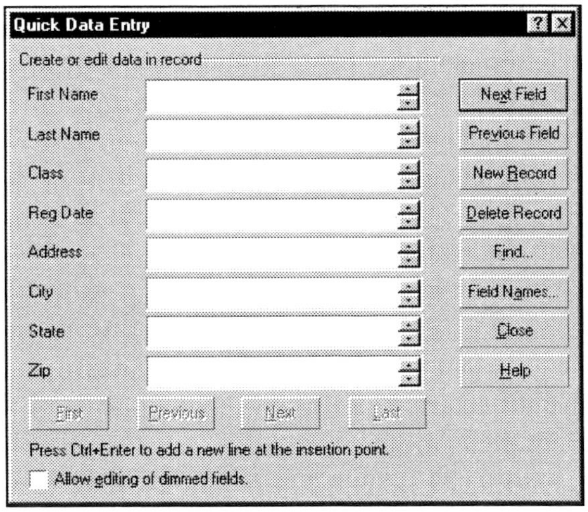

To enter data in the data file and move between records, use the following buttons:

Click this button:	To:
Next Field	move to the next field
Previous Field	move to the previous field
New Record	add the current record and move to a new record
Delete Record	delete the current record
Find	search for a text string
Field Names	display the data source field names for editing
Close	close the Quick Data Entry dialog box
First	move to the first record in the data file
Previous	move to the previous record in the data file
Next	move to the next record in the data file
Last	move to the last record in the data file

TRY IT 5-1 — Creating a Data File

In this exercise, you will define field names for a data file, then enter records into the file.

TIP
The Merge dialog box can be displayed by pressing [Shift] + [F9].

1. **Define the field names for the data file.**

   Click: **Tools** on the menu bar

   Click: **Merge** on the Tools menu

   The Merge dialog box is displayed, as follows:

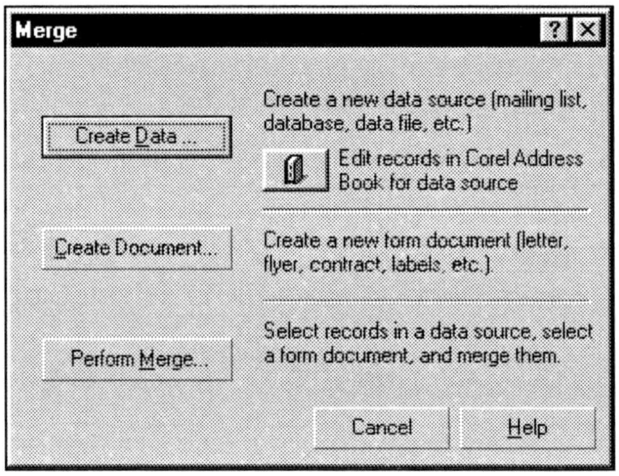

   Click: the **Create Data** button

The Create Data File dialog box is displayed, as follows:

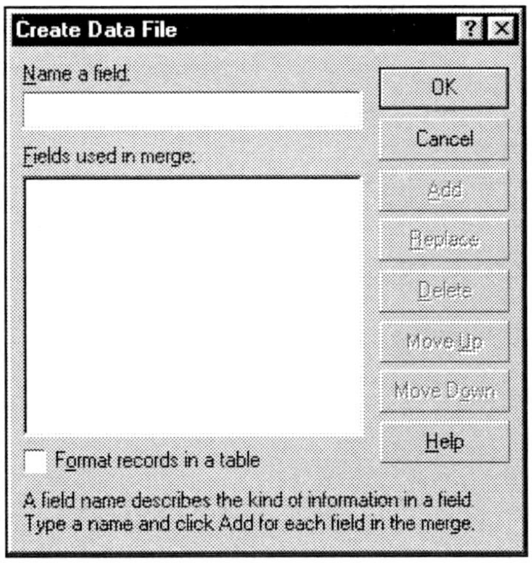

TIP
You can also press [Enter] to add the field to the Fields used in merge list box.

Type: **First Name**

Click: the **Add** button

The first field name is added to the Fields used in merge list box.

Type: **Last Name**

Click: the **Add** button

The next field name is added to the Fields used in merge list box.

2. **On your own, enter the remaining field names, as displayed below:**

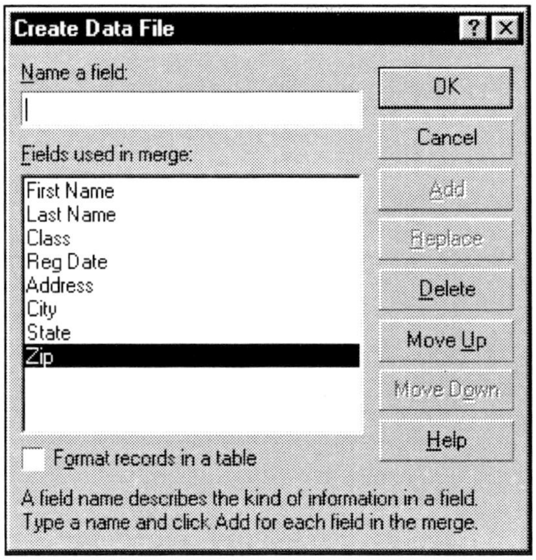

3. **Enter the first record in the data file.**

Click: the **OK** button

The field names are entered, and the Quick Data Entry dialog box is displayed.

Type: **Rose**

Press: **[Enter]**

The first field data is entered in the record, and the insertion point moves to the next field.

Type: **Ruiz**

Press: **[Enter]**

The second field data is entered, and the insertion point is positioned in the next field.

Type: **Sophomore**

Click: the **Next Field** button

Type: **September 9**

Press: **[Enter]**

Type: **765 Pacific Coast Drive**

Press: **[Ctrl] + [Enter]**

A new line is added to the address field data.

Type: **Apt. 772A**

Press: **[Enter]**

Type: **Dublin**

Press: **[Enter]**

Type: **CA**

Press: **[Enter]**

Type: **94589**

The field data for the first record is completed.

Click: the **New Record** button

The first record is entered, and a new, blank record is displayed.

4. On your own, add the following records to the data file:

(Record 2)	(Record 3)
Doris	Nate
Hern	Adams
Senior	Senior
September 7	September 7
150 Dashmond Street	8990 Terrace Lane
Oakland	Berkeley
CA	CA
94911	94745

5. View the records in the data file.

Click: the **First** button

The first record in the data file is displayed.

Click: the **Next** button

The next record is displayed and should look similar to the following:

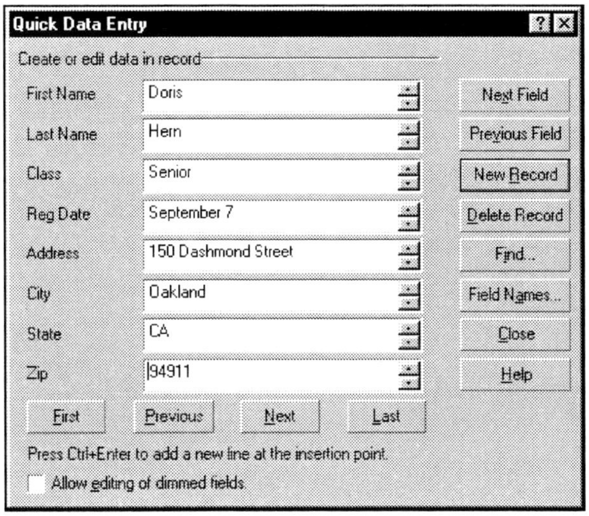

Click: the **Last** button

The last record in the data file is displayed.

6. **Save the records in the data file.**

Click: the **Close** button

A Corel WordPerfect alert box is displayed, prompting you to save the changes to disk.

TIP
The Quick Data Entry dialog box can be redisplayed by clicking the Quick Entry button on the Merge property bar.

Click: the **Yes** button

The Save File dialog box is displayed.

Type: **a:\Students** in the File name text box

Click: the **Save** button

The data file is saved to the data diskette, and the Quick Data Entry dialog box is removed. The data file remains displayed onscreen.

7. **View the data file.**

Press: **[Ctrl] + [Home]**

The insertion point is positioned at the beginning of the document. The document should look similar to the following:

FIELDNAMES(First Name;Last Name;Class;Reg Date;Address;City;State;Zip)ENDRECORD

RoseENDFIELD
RuizENDFIELD
SophomoreENDFIELD
September 9ENDFIELD
765 Pacific Coast Drive
Apt. 772AENDFIELD
DublinENDFIELD
CAENDFIELD
94589ENDFIELD
ENDRECORD

DorisENDFIELD
HernENDFIELD
SeniorENDFIELD
September 7ENDFIELD

NOTE: The field names display at the top of the document window, and each record displays below. Each field is separated by an ENDFIELD merge code, and each record is separated by an ENDRECORD merge code.

Press: **[Ctrl] + [End]**

The insertion point is positioned at the end of the document.

Creating a Form File

For Your Information

The next step in the merge process is creating the form file. You can use an existing document as the form file by simply opening the file and specifying where the field information is to appear. You also have the option of typing a new form file and inserting the field names as you type.

Associating Files

Before merging the form file and the data file, you should associate the two files. Associating the files lets WordPerfect know that they will be used together in the merge operation.

To associate files:

- Open a new document window or retrieve an existing form file.
- Click Tools on the menu bar, then select Merge on the Tools menu.
- Click the Create Document button to display the Create Merge File dialog box, as displayed below:

- Make sure the Use file in active window option is selected, then click the OK button.
- Type the name of the data file you wish to associate in the Associate a data file text box.
- Click the OK button.

Inserting Field Names in a Form File

When a form file is created or opened, WordPerfect displays the Merge property bar to help insert the field names and manage the merge process.

To insert a field name in a form file, you begin by typing the standard text of the document, if necessary, then moving the insertion point to the location where the field information is to be inserted. You then click the Insert Field button on the Merge property bar to display the Insert Field Name or Number dialog box, select a field name from the list box, then click the Insert button. You continue these steps until all the fields are entered.

TRY IT 5–2 — Creating a Form File

In this exercise, you will enter field names in an existing document to create a form file.

1. **On your own, open the file named Register on the data diskette.**

2. **Associate the Students file with the Register file.**

   Click: **Tools** on the menu bar

   Click: **Merge** on the Tools menu

   The Merge dialog box is displayed.

   Click: the **Create Document**

   The Create Merge File dialog box is displayed, as follows:

   NOTE: The Use file in active window option is selected, by default.

   Click: the **OK** button

TIP
You can also browse for the associated data file by clicking the Folder icon attached to the Associate a data file text box.

The Associate Form and Data dialog box is displayed, similar to the following:

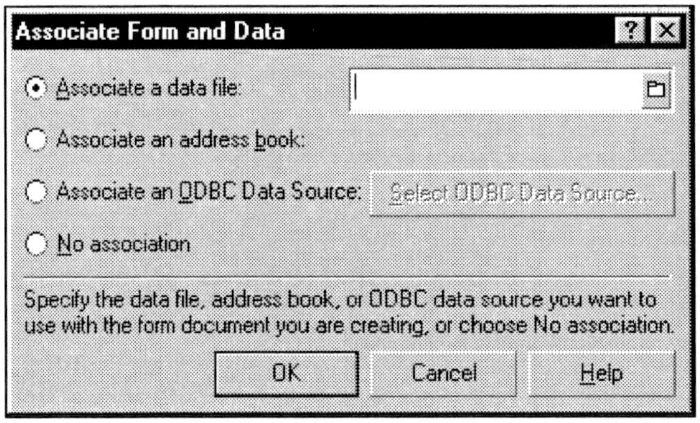

Type: **a:\Students** in the Associate a data file text box

Click: the **OK** button

The two files are associated, and the Merge property bar is displayed at the top of the Register window.

3. Insert the first two field names in the first line of the address block.

Click: the **Insert Field** button on the Merge property bar

The Insert Field Name or Number dialog box is displayed, as follows:

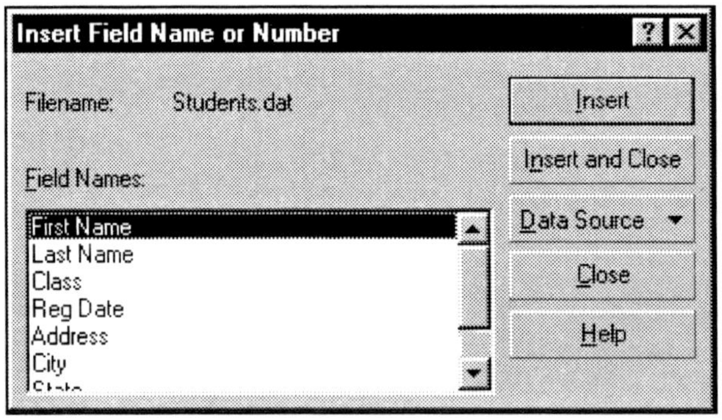

The first field name, "First Name," is highlighted.

Click: the **Insert** button

The field is inserted in the file.

Press: **[Spacebar]**

Click: **Last Name** in the Field Names list box

Click: the **Insert** button

The Last Name field is inserted in the file.

Press: **[Enter]**

The insertion point is positioned on the next line in the address block.

4. **Using a procedure similar to that described above, insert merge fields in the second and third lines of the address block as indicated below:**

FIELD(Address) **FIELD(City), FIELD(State) FIELD(Zip)**

NOTE: Pay particular attention to the spacing between merge fields and to the necessary comma.

5. **Enter the salutation and the appropriate field name.**

Press: **[Enter] [Enter]**

The insertion point is positioned down two lines.

Type: **Dear**

Press: **[Spacebar]**

Click: **First Name** in the Field Names list box

Click: the **Insert** button

Type: **:** (a colon)

The salutation is entered.

6. **Using the same procedure, insert field names in the text of the first sentence, as displayed below:**

> **Registration for the FIELD(Class) class will begin on FIELD(Reg Date) at 9:30 a.m.**

7. **Remove the current dialog box and save the form file.**

Click: the **Close** button

The Insert Field Name or Number dialog box is removed.

Click: the **Save** button

The file is saved, and the beginning of the letter should appear similar to the following:

> FIELD(First Name) FIELD(Last Name)
> FIELD(Address)
> FIELD(City), FIELD(State) FIELD(Zip)
>
> Dear FIELD(First Name):
>
> Registration for the FIELD(Class) class will begin on FIELD(Reg Date) at 9:30 a.m. Please be prompt. You will need to bring the following materials with you to registration:

Completing the Merge Process

For Your Information

Once you have created the data file and the form file, you are ready to merge the two files. You begin the merge process by clicking the Merge button on the Merge property bar, or by clicking Merge on the Tools menu.

Merging the Form File and the Data File

When WordPerfect merges the form and data files, the FIELD codes in the form file are replaced with the field data in the data file, resulting in a third file, which displays onscreen. You have the option of then viewing, editing, or printing this file.

To perform a merge:

- Click the Merge button on the Merge property bar to display the Merge dialog box, as shown below:

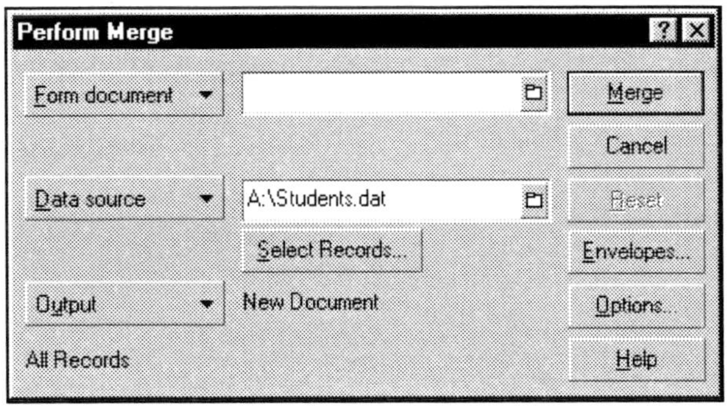

- Click the Merge button.

NOTE: If the data and form files are associated, the appropriate filenames will appear in the Form document and Data source text boxes.

- If necessary, type a filename in the Data source or Output text boxes.

- Click the OK button.

Modifying Merge Options

By default, WordPerfect specifies certain options when the merge is performed. The default merge options include separating each document with a hard page break, printing a single copy of each record, and removing blank lines in a document if no field data is found in the record. You can change these options by clicking the Options button in the Perform Merge dialog box.

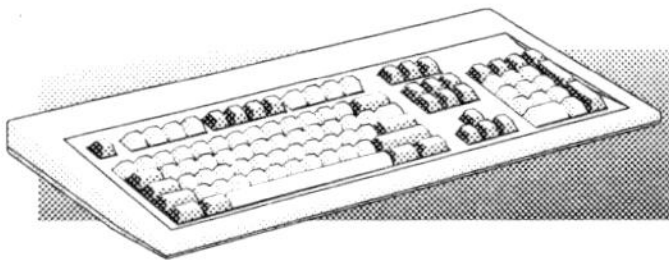

TRY IT 5-3 — Performing a Merge

In this exercise, you will perform a merge.

1. **View both the data and the form files.**

   Click: the **Go to Data** button on the Merge property bar

   The Students document window is displayed.

   Click: the **Go to Form** button on the Merge property bar

   The Register document window is displayed.

2. **Merge the two files. Begin by displaying the Perform Merge dialog box.**

   Click: the **Merge** button on the Merge property bar

   The Perform Merge dialog box is displayed.

   NOTE: Because the two files are associated, A:\Students appears in the Data source text box, and Current Document displays next to Form document. The output file will display in a new document window.

3. **Change the merge options.**

   Click: the **Options** button

   The Perform Merge Options dialog box is displayed, as follows:

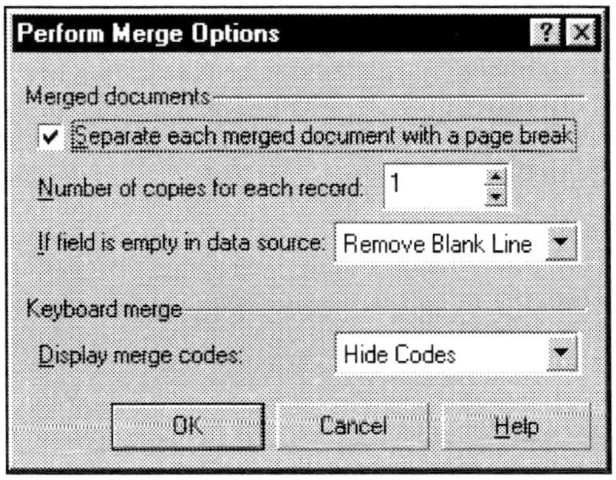

Next: Double-click in the Number of copies for each record text box.

The current selection is highlighted.

Type: **2**

Two documents for each record will be displayed in the output file.

Click: the **OK** button

The Perform Merge dialog box is redisplayed.

4. Complete the merge.

Click: the **Merge** button

The files are merged to a new document window, and the insertion point is positioned at the end of the last letter.

5. Scroll through the document window and examine each record.

Press: **[Ctrl] + [Home]**

The insertion point is positioned at the beginning of the file.

Press: **[Alt] + [Page Down]**

The insertion point is positioned at the top of page two.

NOTE: There should be two pages for each record (six total pages).

Then: On your own, continue to scroll through the file.

6. **Save the letters, then close the file.**

Click: the **Save** button 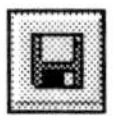

The Save File dialog box is displayed.

Type: **a:\Regltrs** in the File name text box

Click: the **Save** button

The letters are saved.

Click: **File** on the menu bar

Click: **Close** on the File menu

The Register window is redisplayed.

Limiting the Merge Output

For Your Information

In addition to merging all the records in a data file, WordPerfect allows you to merge selected records in the data file by setting up merge conditions. To specify the data to be merged, you begin by clicking the Select Records button in the Perform Merge dialog box.

Merging Selected Records

As your data file grows, you may determine that you only want to merge records that match certain conditions; for example, you might limit a merge operation to records containing a specific city or zip code.

To merge selected records only:

- Display the Merge dialog box, then click the Merge button in the Perform Merge section.
- Click the Select Records button to display the following:

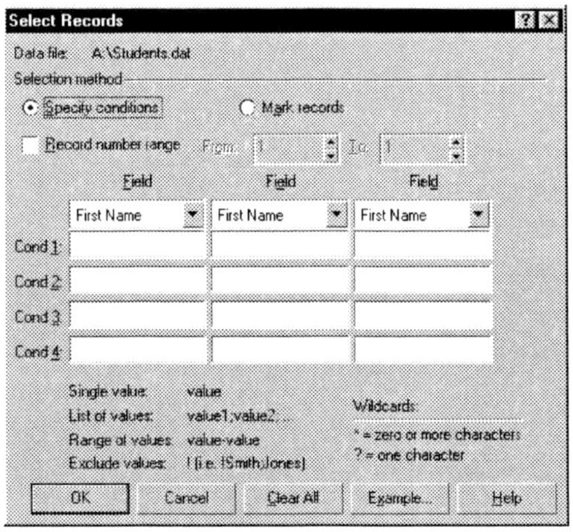

- Expand the first Field drop-down list box and select a field.
- Click in the Cond 1 text box and type a criterion.
- Click the OK button to return to the Perform Merge dialog box.
- Click the OK button to merge the selected records.

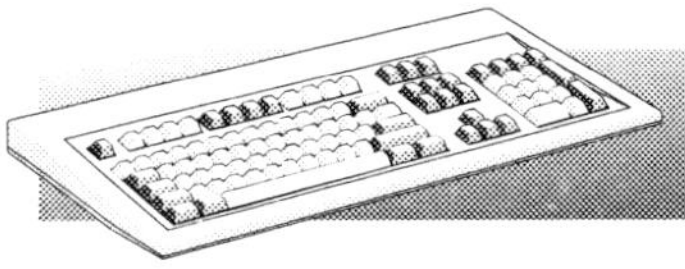

TRY IT 5–4 — Modifying the Merge Output

In this exercise, you will merge only records with "Senior" in the Class field.

1. Begin another merge operation.

First: Make sure the Register document is active.

Click: the **Merge** button on the Merge property bar

The Perform Merge dialog box is displayed.

2. Modify the merge options.

Click: the **Options** button

The Perform Merge Options dialog box is displayed.

Next: Double-click in the Number of copies for each record text box.

Type: **1**

Click: the **OK** button

The merge options are modified.

3. Define the merge conditions.

Click: the **Select Records** button

The Select Records dialog box is displayed.

Next: Expand the first Field drop-down list box and select **Class**.

The field name is selected. The Class field will be used as the first selection condition.

Then: Click in the Cond 1 text box.

Type: **Senior**

The condition is entered, and the dialog box should look similar to the following:

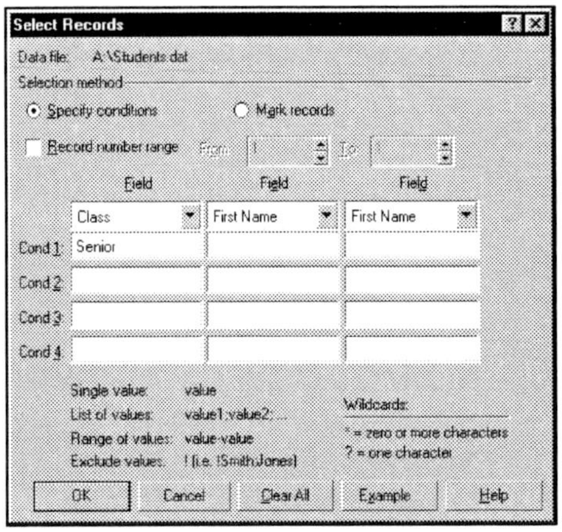

NOTE: WordPerfect will merge only records with "Senior" in the Class field.

Click: the **OK** button

The Perform Merge dialog box is redisplayed.

4. **Perform the merge operation, then view the results.**

Click: the **Merge** button

The records are merged to a new document window.

Press: **[Ctrl] + [Home]**

The insertion point is positioned in the first record with "Senior" in the Class field.

5. **Close the document window without saving.**

Click: **File** on the menu bar

Click: **Close** on the File menu

Click: the **No** button

The document window is closed.

6. **On your own, close the Register file without saving.**

Sorting Records in a Data File

For Your Information

When creating merge documents, you may find it advantageous to have your data file organized in a particular manner. For example, for a large mailing, you might want to have the records ordered by zip code. This can be accomplished by clicking Sort on the Tools menu, or by clicking the Options button on the Merge property bar and then selecting Sort.

Using Sort

The *Sort* feature allows you to arrange information in a document alphabetically or numerically in either ascending or descending order. In addition to providing a convenient method for sorting lists and tables, this feature gives you the ability to organize records in a data file by a specific field, by a word on a specific line within a field, by multiple fields, or by multiple words within fields.

To sort a data file, you begin by defining the sort key. The *sort key* is the field on which a sort operation is performed. Key 1, the primary sort key, is used to initially sort all records.

Within each sort key, you specify the following:

Type	indicates whether the key is alpha or numeric.
Sort Order	determines if the key will be sorted in ascending or descending order.
Line	indicates the line on which you wish to sort.
Field	indicates the field on which you wish to sort, with 1 being the first field, 2 being the second field, and so on.
Word	indicates the position of the word on which you wish to sort, with 1 being the first word, 2 being the second word, and so on.

Sorting the Data File

To sort a data file, you begin by displaying the Sort dialog box, then editing the sort definition.

To sort a data file:

- Click Tools on the menu bar.
- Click Sort on the Tools menu to display the following dialog box:

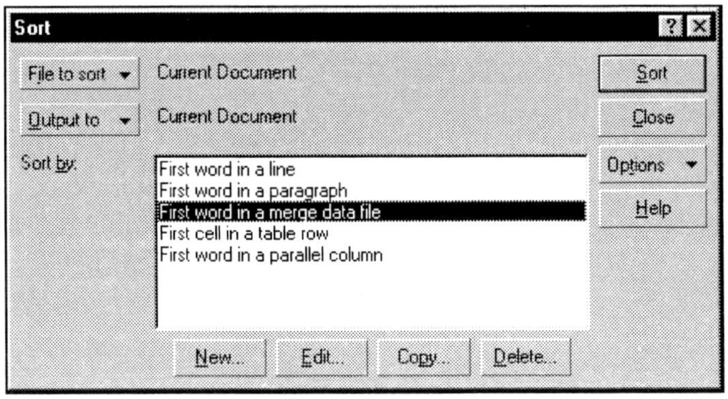

- In the Sort by list box, select the sort definition to edit.
- Click the Edit button.
- Select the desired field, line, or word.
- Click the OK button.
- Click the Sort button.

From the Edit Sort dialog box, you can also modify the type of sort and the sort order by expanding the Type and Sort order list boxes, respectively.

TRY IT 5–5 — Sorting a Data File

In this exercise, you will sort the records in the Students data file.

TIP
You can also display the Sort dialog box by pressing [Alt] + [F9].

1. Begin the sort operation.

Click: **Tools** on the menu bar

Click: **Sort** on the Tools menu

The Sort dialog box is displayed, as follows:

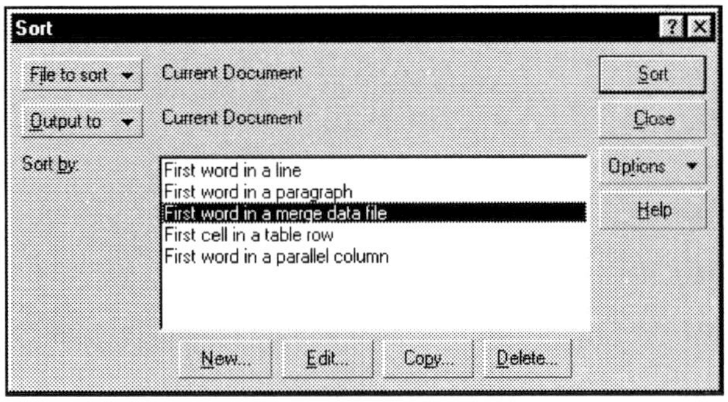

NOTE: First word in a merge data file is the default.

Click: the **Edit** button

The Edit Sort dialog box is displayed, as follows:

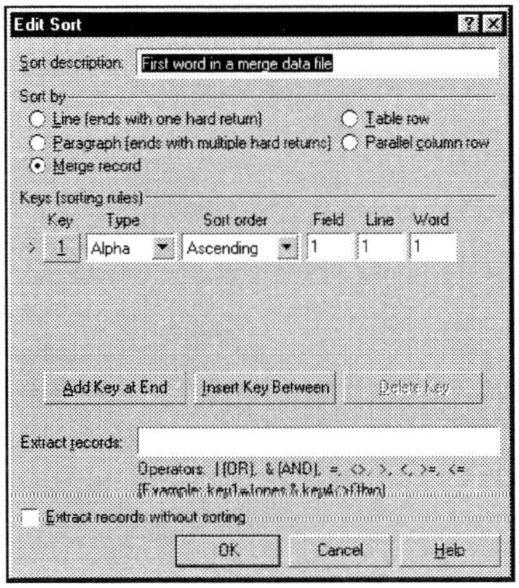

2. Specify the sorting criteria.

First: In the Keys (sorting rules) section, double-click in the Field text box, then type 2.

NOTE: Field 2 is the Last Name field.

Click: the **OK** button

Click: the **Sort** button

The records are sorted by last name in ascending order.

3. Sort the records by zip code in descending order.

Click: the **Options** button on the Merge property bar

Click: **Sort** on the Options menu

Click: the **Edit** button

Next: Double-click in the Field text box, then type **8**.

NOTE: Field 8 is the Zip Code field.

Then: Click the Type list box, and select **Numeric**.

Next: Click the Sort order list box, and select **Descending**.

The Type and Sort order options are entered.

Click: the **OK** button

Click: the **Sort** button

The records are sorted in descending order by zip code.

4. On your own, close the Students file without saving.

Creating Envelopes

For Your Information

One of WordPerfect's most useful features is the Envelope command on the Format menu. Using this option, you can address and print an envelope without setting up any special merge fields. This is useful when you need to address only a few envelopes at a time.

Creating an Envelope

To enter the mailing address and return address on an envelope, click Envelope on the Format menu. If you are creating an envelope to go with a letter currently displayed onscreen, WordPerfect will automatically select the mailing address and insert it in the appropriate text box.

To create an envelope based on the current document:

- Make sure that the mailing address in the current document is followed by at least two hard returns.
- Click Format on the menu bar.
- Click Envelope on the Format menu to display the following:

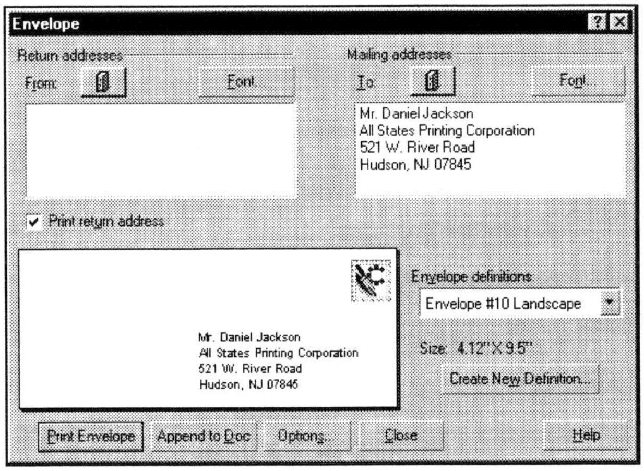

- Make sure your printer is set up to print envelopes.
- Click the Print Envelope button.

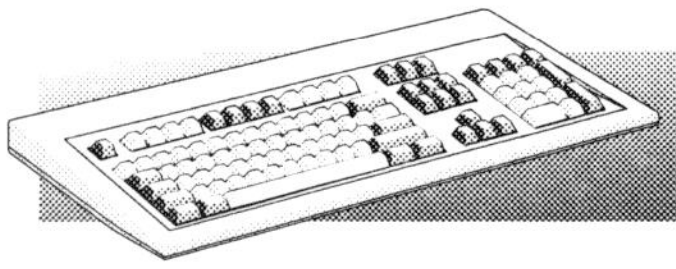

TRY IT 5–6 — Creating and Printing an Envelope

In this exercise, you will create and print an envelope using the Envelope command.

1. On your own, open the file named Printers.

2. Create an envelope using the mailing address in the document.

Click: **Format** on the menu bar

Click: **Envelope** on the Format menu

The Envelope dialog box is displayed, as follows:

TIP
If the address is not followed by two hard returns, WordPerfect will not recognize it as an address.

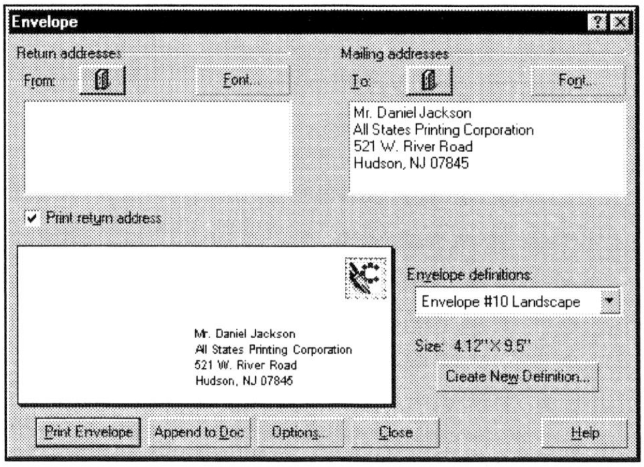

NOTE: The address in the current document is displayed in the Mailing addresses text box and on the sample envelope.

3. Print the envelope.

NOTE: If your printer is not set up to print envelopes, simply click the **Close** button.

Click: the **Print Envelope** button

The Envelope dialog box is closed, and the envelope is printed.

NOTE: Depending on your printer, you may have to manually feed the envelope.

4. **On your own, close the document window without saving.**

Summary of Lesson 5

To create a data file:

- Click **Tools** on the menu bar.
- Click **Merge** on the Tools menu.
- Click the **Create Data** button.
- Click **Use file in active window** to use the open document window, or click **New document window** to create the data file in a new document window, and click the **OK** button.
- Type a field name in the Name a field text box.
- Click the **Add** button.
- Continue adding field names using the above steps until all the field names have been added.

To associate files:

- Open a new document window or retrieve an existing form file.
- Click **Tools** on the menu bar.
- Click **Merge** on the Tools menu.
- Click the **Create Document** button to display the Create Merge File dialog box.
- Make sure the Use file in active window option is selected, then click the **OK** button.
- Type the name of the data file you wish to associate in the Associate a data file text box.
- Click the **OK** button.

To perform a merge:

- Click the **Merge** button on the Merge property bar.
- Click the **Merge** button.
- If necessary, type a filename in the Form document, Data source, or Output text boxes.
- Click the **OK** button.

To merge selected records only:

- Display the Merge dialog box, then click the **Merge** button in the Perform Merge section.
- Click the **Select Records** button.
- Expand the first Field drop-down list box and select a field.
- Click in the Cond 1 text box and type a criterion.
- Click the **OK** button to return to the Perform Merge dialog box.
- Click the **OK** button to merge the selected records.

To sort a data file:

- Click **Tools** on the menu bar.
- Click **Sort** on the Tools menu.
- In the Sort by list box, select the sort definition to edit.
- Click the **Edit** button.
- Select the desired field, line, or word.
- Click the **OK** button.
- Click the **Sort** button.

To create an envelope based on the current document:

- Make sure that the mailing address in the current document is followed by at least two hard returns.
- Click **Format** on the menu bar.
- Click **Envelope** on the Format menu.
- Make sure your printer is set up to print envelopes.
- Click the **Print Envelope** button.

Practice Exercise — Lesson 5

1. Create a data file with the following field names:

FirstName
LastName
Address1
Address2
Prize

2. Add the following records to the data file:

Paul	Patty	Jay
Cameron	Jones	Thomas
4358 W. Cholla Street	15543 E. Mountainside	4671 N. Sequoia
Glendale, AZ 85208	Phoenix, AZ 84044	Phoenix, AZ 85224
2,500	2,100	1,500

3. Save the data file with the name Names.

4. Open the file Work2-5.WPD in a new document window, then associate the Names file with Work 2-5.WPD. (Hint: Click Merge on the Tools menu, then click the Create Document button.)

5. Insert the appropriate field names in the address block and body of the form file by replacing the information in brackets.

6. Save the current version of the form file.

7. Merge the form file and all the records in the data file to a new document.

8. Save the resulting letters with the filename Mrgletrs, then close the document windows.

9. Display the Names file, then sort the data file by last name in descending order.

10. Save the file, then close all open windows.

Lesson 6 Creating Macros/Using Templates

Lesson Objectives

By the end of this lesson, you will be able to create and execute macros. You will also learn how to create a template and use a WordPerfect interactive template.

You will learn how to:

- record and play macros
- edit a macro
- create a simple template

Creating Macros

For Your Information

A *macro* is a recorded series of keystrokes that, when executed, performs one or more operations. Using the Macro command on the Tools menu, you can automate such repetitive tasks as:

- saving and/or printing a document
- inserting dates
- setting up page layout formats
- entering often-used text
- creating a letterhead or a business letter ending
- defining columns

WordPerfect comes equipped with its own set of macros, which can be used to execute a variety of tasks.

Planning a Macro

Before recording a macro, you should carefully plan the series of keystrokes you want to automate. It is usually a good idea to jot down an outline that lists:

- the sequence in which the various operations are to occur
- the commands and actions for performing each operation

Additionally, it is important to note that the macro recorder does not record mouse movements in a document window, so you must use the keyboard to select text and move the insertion point. You can, however, use the mouse to choose commands.

Recording a Macro

To begin recording a macro, you select Macro on the Tools menu, then click Record on the Macro submenu. WordPerfect records macros in a command language, which means that the results of the keystrokes, not the actual steps, are recorded.

When recording a macro, you begin by naming the macro. If you do not include an extension, WordPerfect adds the default extension .wcm. If you do not specify a path, the file is stored in the default macro directory. After the macro is named, you begin entering the operations you want recorded. The insertion point will appear as a circle with a line through it, and the message "Macro Record" displays in the application bar when recording a macro.

To record a macro:

- Click Tools on the menu bar.
- Select Macro on the Tools menu.
- Click Record on the Macro submenu to display the following:

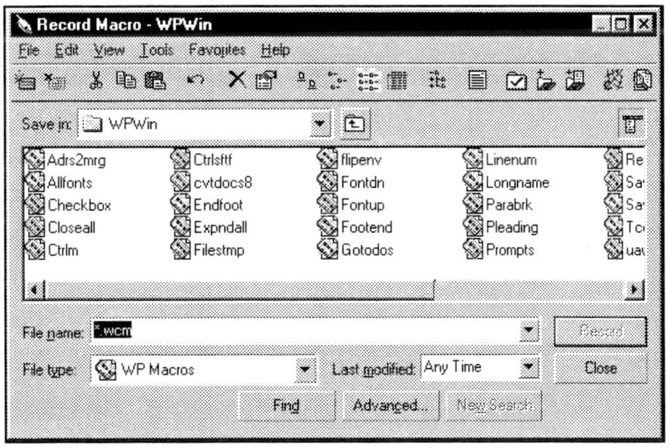

- Type a name for the macro in the File name text box.
- Click the Record button.
- In the document window, perform the desired operations.

To turn off the macro recorder, click Record on the Macro submenu.

Playing a Macro

By default, WordPerfect inserts the last macro you played on the Macro submenu. To play that macro, click Macro on the Tools menu, then select the macro. You can also play macros that have been previously created and are stored on disk. When you execute a macro, the results of the keystrokes you recorded are played back.

To play an existing macro:

- Position the insertion point where you want to begin the macro.
- Click Tools on the menu bar.
- Click Macro on the Tools menu.
- Click Play on the Macro submenu to display the following:

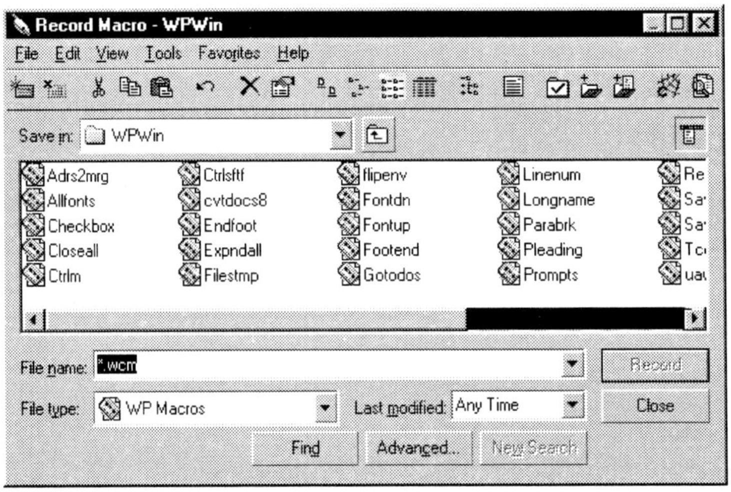

- Type the macro name in the File name text box.
- Click the Play button.

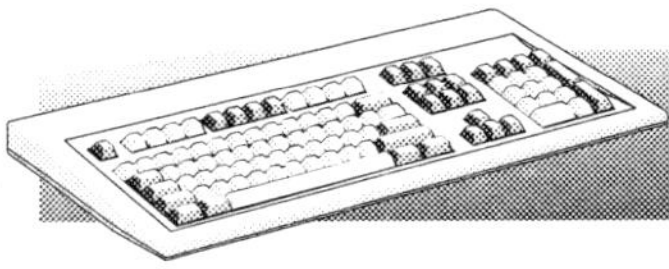

TRY IT 6–1 — Recording and Playing Macros

In this exercise, you will create and execute three macros.

TIP
The macro recorder can be turned on and off by pressing [Ctrl] + [F10].

1. **Record a macro that can be used to end a business letter. Begin by turning on the macro recorder.**

Click: **Tools** on the menu bar

Select: **Macro** on the Tools menu

Click: **Record** on the Macro submenu

The Record Macro dialog box is displayed, as follows:

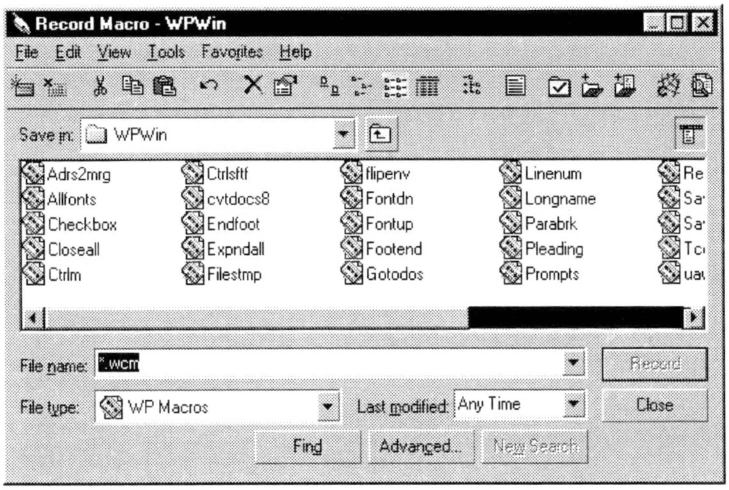

Type: **a:\letend** in the File name text box

Click: the **Record** button

The insertion point is displayed as a circle with a line through it, and "Macro Record" is displayed in the status bar.

2. **Record the steps for a business letter ending.**

Type: **Please call if you have any questions.**

Press: **[Enter] [Enter] [Enter]**

Type: **Sincerely,**

Press: **[Enter] [Enter]**

Type: **JoAnne Donovan**

Press: **[Enter]**

Type: **Dean of Students**

The letter ending text is entered.

3. **Turn off the macro recorder, then delete the text you typed.**

Click: **Tools** on the menu bar

Select: **Macro** on the Tools menu

Click: **Record** on the Macro submenu

The macro recorder is turned off and the macro is saved.

Next: Select the text in the document window.

Press: **[Delete]**

The text is deleted.

4. Create a macro for a business letterhead. Begin by naming the macro and changing the margins.

Click: **Tools** on the menu bar

Select: **Macro** on the Tools menu

Click: **Record** on the Macro submenu

The Record Macro dialog box is displayed.

Type: **a:\ltrhead** in the File name text box

Click: the **Record** button

The macro recorder is turned on.

Click: **Format** on the menu bar

Click: **Margins** on the Format menu

Type: **1.5** in the Left text box

Press: **[Tab]**

Type: **1.5** in the Right text box

Press: **[Tab]**

Type: **3** in the Top text box

Press: **[Tab]**

Type: **.5** in the Bottom text box

Click: the **OK** button

The margin settings for the letterhead are set.

5. **Type the text of the letterhead.**

Type: **BLACKBERRY BUSINESS COLLEGE**

Press: **[Enter]**

Type: **1223 E. College Lane**

Press: **[Enter]**

Type: **San Francisco, CA 90012**

Press: **[Enter]**

6. **Center the text, insert the date, then turn off the macro recorder.**

Click: **Edit** on the menu bar

Select: **Select** on the Edit menu

Click: **All** on the Select submenu

The text is selected.

Click: **Format** on the menu bar

Select: **Line** on the Format menu

Click: **Center** on the Line submenu

The selected text is centered.

Press: **[Ctrl] + [End]**

The insertion point is positioned at the end of the document.

Press: **[Enter] [Enter] [Enter] [Enter]**

Click: **Insert** on the menu bar

Click: **Date/Time** on the Insert menu

Click: **Keep the inserted date current**

Click: the **Insert** button

The date code is inserted in the letterhead.

Press: **[Enter] [Enter] [Enter]**

The letterhead is completed, and the document should look similar to the following:

Click: **Tools** on the menu bar

Select: **Macro** on the Tools menu

Click: **Record** on the Macro submenu

The macro recorder is turned off.

7. On your own, delete the text and codes in the document window.

8. **Create a macro that will convert lowercase text to uppercase.**

Type: **this is a test**

Then: Select the text you just typed.

Press: **[Ctrl] + [F10]**

The Record Macro dialog box is displayed.

Type: **a:\upper** in the File name text box

Click: the **Record** button

The macro recorder is turned on.

Click: **Edit** on the menu bar

Select: **Convert Case** on the Edit menu

Click: **UPPERCASE** on the Convert Case submenu

The selected text is converted to uppercase.

9. **Turn off the macro, then delete the text you typed.**

Press: **[Ctrl] + [F10]**

The macro recorder is turned off.

Press: **[Delete]**

The selected text is deleted.

10. **Execute the macros you just recorded to create a business letter. Begin by executing the letterhead macro and typing the body of the letter.**

Click: **Tools** on the menu bar

Select: **Macro** on the Tools menu

Click: **Play** on the Macro submenu

The Play Macro dialog box is displayed, as follows:

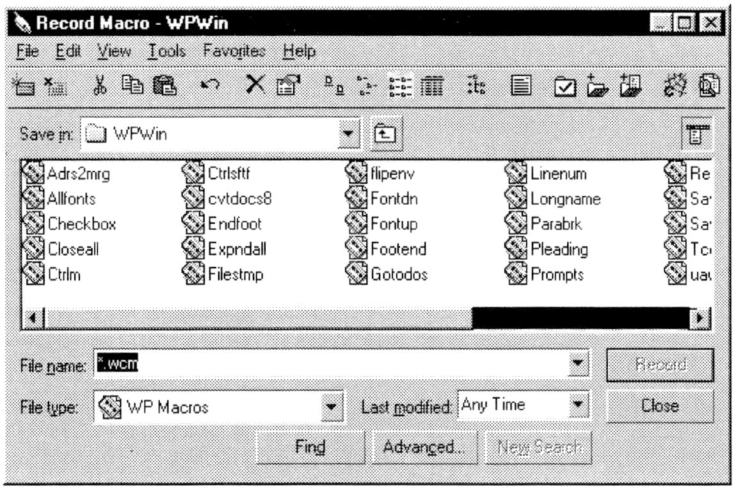

Type:	**a:\ltrhead** in the File name text box
Click:	the **Play** button

The letterhead macro is played.

Type:	**Dear Tom Hansen:**
Press:	**[Enter] [Enter]**
Type:	**Congratulations! You have been accepted to Blackberry Business College. Registration begins Monday the 25th at 1:00 P.M. Please bring a picture ID.**
Press:	**[Enter] [Enter]**

11. Execute the letter ending macro to complete the letter.

Press:	**[Alt] + [F10]**

The Play Macro dialog box is displayed.

Type:	**a:\letend**

Click: the **Play** button

The ending to the letter is displayed, and the document should look similar to the following:

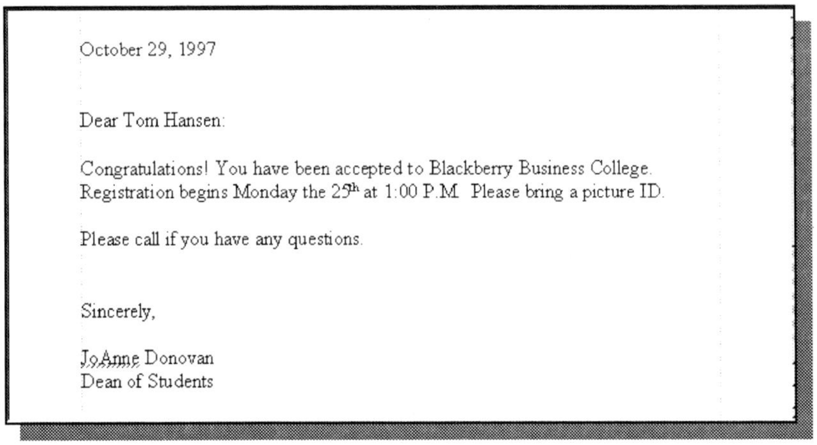

October 29, 1997

Dear Tom Hansen:

Congratulations! You have been accepted to Blackberry Business College. Registration begins Monday the 25th at 1:00 P.M. Please bring a picture ID.

Please call if you have any questions.

Sincerely,

JoAnne Donovan
Dean of Students

12. Use the upper macro to change the case of text in the letter.

First: Select the word "Congratulations."

Click: **Tools** on the menu bar

Select: **Macro** on the Tools menu

Click: **Play** on the Macro submenu

Type: **a:\upper**

Click: the **Play** button

The macro is executed, and the text is capitalized.

Press: **[Down Arrow]**

The text is deselected.

13. Close the document window without saving.

Editing and Deleting Macros

For Your Information

When a macro is no longer useful, it can simply be deleted. To modify a macro, however, you must use the WordPerfect macro language. While a detailed discussion of this language is beyond the scope of this course, you will be introduced to a simple instruction.

Editing a Macro

There are two methods for editing a macro. If the macro is fairly simple, the easiest way to correct a problem is to re-record the entire macro. If the macro is more complex, you can edit the macro instructions.

To edit a macro:

- Click Tools on the menu bar.
- Select Macro on the Tools menu.
- Click Edit on the Macro submenu.
- Type the name of the macro you wish to edit in the File name text box.
- Click the Edit button to display the following:

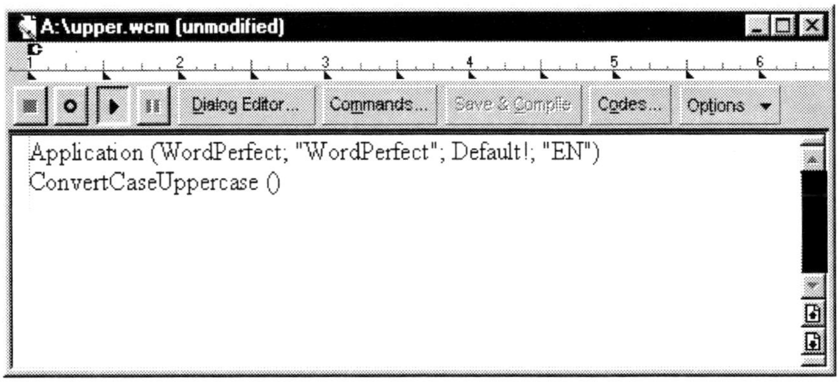

- Make corrections as necessary.
- Close the macro.

Deleting Macros

The macros you create are automatically stored for use at all times. If you decide you no longer need a macro, you can simply delete it. To delete a macro, display the Edit Macro dialog box, locate the desired macro, then click the Delete button on the toolbar.

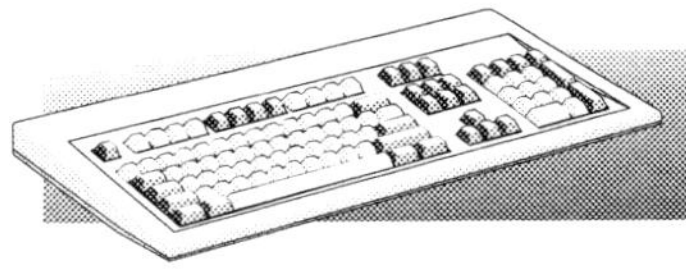

TRY IT 6–2 — Editing a Macro

In this exercise, you will edit and then delete a macro.

1. **Edit the upper macro. Begin by displaying the macro instructions.**

Click: **Tools** on the menu bar

Select: **Macro** on the Tools menu

Click: **Edit** on the Macro submenu

The Edit Macro dialog box is displayed, as follows:

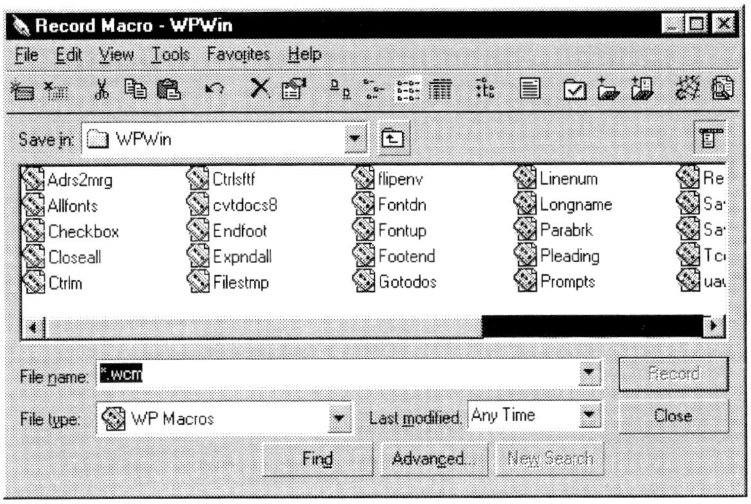

Type: **a:\upper** in the File name text box

Click: the **Edit** button

The macro instructions for the upper macro are displayed, and the Macro property bar is positioned at the top of the document window.

Press: **[Ctrl] + [End]**

The insertion point is positioned at the end of the instructions.

Type: **PosLineDown()**

The instruction is entered and should look similar to the following:

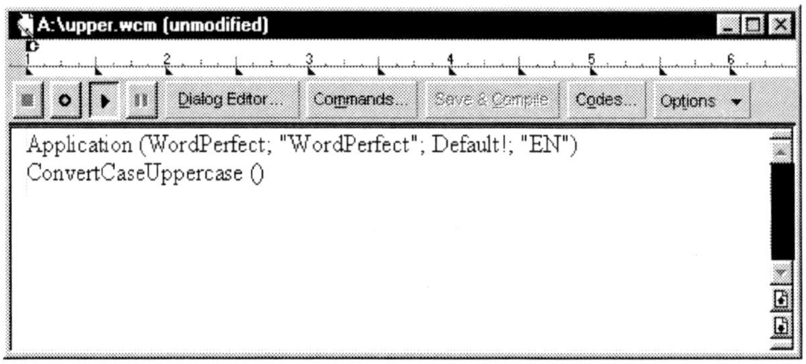

NOTE: The new instruction will move the insertion point down one line, thereby deselecting the text, when the macro is executed.

Click: the **Save & Compile** button on the Macro property bar

The macro is automatically saved and recompiled.

Click: the **Options** button on the Macro property bar

The Options drop-down list is expanded.

Click: **Close Macro**

The macro window is closed.

2. **Run the updated macro.**

Type: **this is a test of the new macro**

Press: **[Enter]**

Next: Select the entire line you just typed.

Press: **[Alt] + [F10]**

The Play Macro dialog box is displayed.

Type: **a:\upper** in the File name text box

Click: the **Play** button

The macro is run, and the text is capitalized, then deselected. The insertion point is displayed below the text.

3. Delete the upper macro.

Click: **Tools** on the menu bar

Select: **Macro** on the Tools menu

Click: **Edit** on the Macro submenu

The Edit Macro dialog box is displayed.

Next: Expand the Look in drop-down list box, then click the floppy drive icon, if necessary.

Click: **upper**

The macro is selected.

Click: the **Delete** button  on the toolbar

An alert box is displayed prompting you to delete the macro.

Click: the **Yes** button

The macro is deleted.

Click: the **Close** button

The Edit Macro dialog box is closed.

4. On your own, close the document window without saving the file.

Working with Templates

For Your Information

Every file you create in WordPerfect is based on a template. A *template* is a file that contains boilerplate text, formatting, and styles, and can be used over and over again to create similar documents.

The default WordPerfect template is called *WordPerfect Document*, and any new file you create is based on this template unless otherwise specified. WordPerfect also comes with its own set of templates. Some of these templates are interactive, which means that they feature built-in prompts that allow you to quickly enter variable information in the template. You can create templates of your own, modify existing templates, or use the templates that WordPerfect provides.

Creating a Template

To begin creating a template, you open a new template file, set formatting characteristics, and enter the boilerplate text. When a template is created or edited, the Template property bar is displayed.

To create a template:

- Click File on the menu bar.
- Click New on the File menu.
- Click the Options button.
- Click Create WP Template in the expanded list box to display a new document window and the Template property bar.
- Type the desired boilerplate text in the document window.
- Click the Close button on the property bar.
- Click the Yes button.
- Type a description of the template in the Description text box.
- In the Template name text box, enter a template name.
- In the Template group list box, select the group to which the new template belongs.
- Click the OK button.

Using a Template

To use an existing template, you begin by clicking New on the File menu. The default template is highlighted in the Select template list box.

To use a template:

- Click File on the menu bar.
- Click New on the File menu.
- Click the desired template group in the Template group drop-down list box.
- Click the desired template in the Select template list box.
- Click the Create button.

TRY IT 6–3 — Creating a Simple Template

In this exercise, you will create a template for a boilerplate memo.

1. Create a new template file.

Click: **File** on the menu bar

Click: **New** on the File menu

The New dialog box is displayed, as follows:

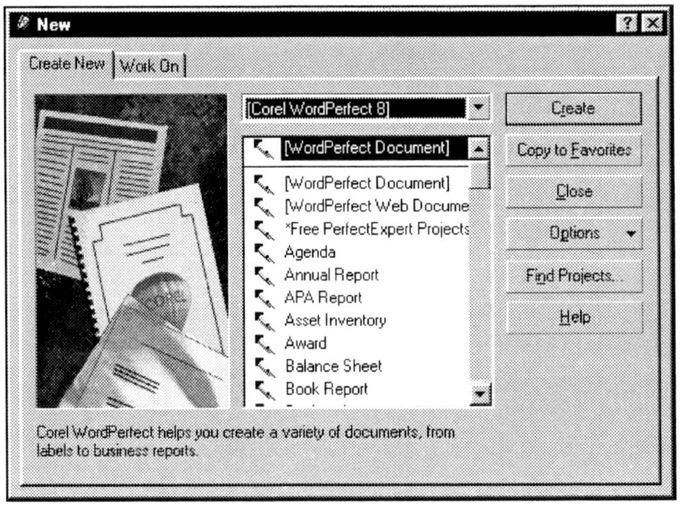

Click: the **Options** button

The Options drop-down list is expanded.

Click: **Create WP Template**

A new document window is opened, and the Template property bar is displayed.

2. **Set the margins for the memo.**

Click: **Format** on the menu bar

Click: **Margins** on the Layout menu

Type: **2** in the Left text box

Press: **[Tab]**

Type: **2** in the Right text box

Press: **[Tab]**

Type: **1.5** in the Top text box

Press: **[Tab]**

Type: **.5** in the Bottom text box

Click: the **OK** button

TIP
The Margins dialog box can also be displayed by pressing [Ctrl] + [F8].

3. **Enter the boilerplate text for the memo. Begin by entering the two-line memo heading, then center and bold the text.**

Type: **MEMORANDUM**

Press: **[Enter]**

Type: **THE BLACKBERRY VINE**

Press: **[Enter]**

Next: Select the text in the document window.

Click: the **Bold** button on the toolbar

Then: Click the **Justification** button on the property bar.

The Justification drop-down list is expanded.

Click: **Center**

The heading is centered and bolded.

4. **Enter the memo text, including a date code that will automatically insert the data in the memo when executed.**

Press: **[Ctrl] + [End]**

The text is deselected, and the insertion point is positioned at the end of the file.

Press: **[Enter] [Enter] [Enter]**

Type: **TO:**

Press: **[Tab] [Tab]**

Press: **[Enter] [Enter]**

Type: **FROM:**

Press: **[Tab] [Enter] [Enter]**

Type: **DATE:**

Press: **[Tab]**

Click: **Insert** on the menu bar

Click: **Date/Time** on the Insert menu

Click: **Keep the inserted date current**

Click: the **Insert** button

The current date is inserted in the document.

Press: **[Enter] [Enter]**

Type: **SUBJECT:**

Press: **[Tab] [Enter] [Enter]**

The boilerplate text is entered.

5. **Save the memo template.**

Click: the **Close** button  on the Template property bar

A Corel WordPerfect alert box is displayed.

Click: the **Yes** button

The Save Template dialog box is displayed, as follows:

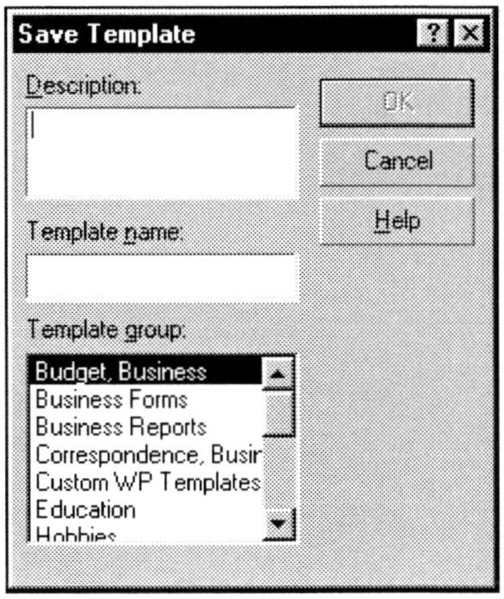

Type: **Standard Memo** in the Description text box

Press: **[Tab]**

Type: **memofile** in the Template name text box

Click: **Business Forms** in the Template group list box

Click: the **OK** button

The template file is saved, and the document window is cleared.

TIP
You can also double-click the template name to create a document.

6. **Use the memofile template to create a memo.**

Click: **File** on the menu bar

Click: **New** on the File menu

The New dialog box is displayed.

Next: Expand the Template group drop-down list box.

Click: **Business Forms** in the expanded list box

The templates in the Business Forms group are listed in the Select template list box.

Click: **Standard Memo**

Click: the **Create** button

A new document is created from the new template. The insertion point is displayed at the beginning of the file.

7. **On your own, use the arrow keys to position the insertion point at the text input locations, and type a sample memo.**

8. **On your own, close the document window without saving.**

Summary of Lesson 6

To record a macro:

- Click **Tools** on the menu bar.
- Select **Macro** on the Tools menu.
- Click **Record** on the Macro submenu.
- Type a name for the macro in the File name text box.
- Click the **Record** button.
- In the document window, perform the operations you wish to record.

To play an existing macro:

- Position the insertion point where you want to begin the macro.
- Click **Tools** on the menu bar.
- Click **Macro** on the Tools menu.
- Click **Play** on the Macro submenu.
- Type the macro name in the File name text box.
- Click the **Play** button.

To edit a macro:

- Click **Tools** on the menu bar.
- Click **Macro** on the Tools menu.
- Click **Edit** on the Macro submenu.
- Type the name of the macro you wish to edit in the File name text box.
- Click the **Edit** button.
- Make corrections as necessary.
- Click the **Close** button.

To create a template:

- Click **File** on the menu bar.
- Click **New** on the File menu.
- Click the **Options** button.
- Click **Create WP Template** in the expanded list box to display a new document window and the Template property bar.
- Type the desired boilerplate text in the document window.
- Click the **Close** button on the property bar.
- Click the **Yes** button.
- Type a description of the template in the Description text box.
- In the Template name text box, enter a template name.
- In the Template group list box, select the group to which the new template belongs.
- Click the **OK** button.

To use a template:

- Click **File** on the menu bar.
- Click **New** on the File menu.
- Click the desired template group in the Template group list box.
- Click the desired template in the Select template list box.
- Click the **Select** button.

Practice Exercise — Lesson 6

1. If necessary, start WordPerfect.
2. Create your own personal letterhead macro named MYLTRHD with your name and address centered at the top of the page.
3. Select and delete the text.
4. Run the MYLTRHD macro.
5. Delete the MYLTRHD macro.
6. View the report in full page view, then print the document if desired.
7. Close all document windows without saving.
8. Exit WordPerfect for Windows.

Glossary

alert box — a window in which an error message, warning, or prompt for additional information is displayed.

application — software used for a general-purpose operation, such as word processing, database, spreadsheet, desktop publishing, or graphic illustration.

backup — a copy of a file or an entire disk for use in the event the working copy becomes lost or damaged.

button — a graphic device inside a dialog box that sets an option or executes an operation when it is selected or "clicked" with a mouse.

central processing unit (CPU) — a microchip that performs calculations and serves as the computer's "brain" by coordinating the system's processing of information.

clicking — the action of pressing and releasing a mouse button when the mouse pointer is positioned over a specific screen item.

clipboard — in Windows, a temporary storage area designed to hold a text block or graphic.

Control-menu box — an element of an application or document window. The Control-menu box is used to perform various window operations.

copy — a duplication of a text block or a document file. Also, an operation that involves copying text from a document and placing it in a temporary storage location.

data — any alphanumeric information that is entered into, manipulated, or stored by a computer.

default — a preset or automatic setting established the first time a software application is loaded into a computer's memory (RAM).

dialog box — a window that appears during command execution and displays current information and options that can be selected before completing a command.

direction keys — keys used to move an insertion point or similar object up, down, left, or right.

directory	a special area on disks that is generally used to group related files.
dragging	the action of positioning the mouse pointer over a specific screen item, pressing and holding down a mouse button, and moving the mouse pointer to another screen location.
edit	an operation that revises text, including content and formatting changes.
[Enter] key	a key used to send information to the computer. This key is synonymous with the "return" key on a typewriter; however, when typing text, it is used to designate the end of a paragraph, not the end of every line.
error message	information that appears onscreen to inform a user that an error has occurred.
font	a specific family of type or character style whose availability is dependent on the printer device connected to the computer system.
format	an operating system command that is used to prepare a new diskette so that information can be written to and read from it. Also, the appearance of text and other elements on the page.
function keys	a set of keys labeled "F" and a number (1 through 12) that are generally used as shortcut methods to execute commands.
Help	a utility that contains information about an application's various commands, operations, and features.
icon	a graphic device displayed onscreen that executes a command, adjusts an application setting, or otherwise performs a specific operation when "clicked" with a mouse
macro	a series of stored keystrokes that can be used to automate an application-specific task, thereby eliminating repetitive keystrokes.
margin	the area between the edge of the paper and the text of the document.
menu	an onscreen list of available options, common to all Windows applications.
menu bar	the horizontal bar just below the title bar. The menu bar contains command names that refer to pull-down menus.

Microsoft Windows an operating environment developed by Microsoft Corporation. The Windows interface allows multiple software applications to be run simultaneously, each operating in its own window.

mode a particular set of program features or characteristics that influence a program operation. For example, pressing [Caps Lock] generally switches any word processing application to uppercase mode.

mouse a hand-held hardware device equipped with one or more buttons that is moved across a flat surface to freely move an object called a *mouse pointer* around the computer screen. The mouse is used to select other screen items that execute commands or perform various operations.

mouse pointer an onscreen object used to point at other screen objects and controlled by moving a mouse across a flat surface.

option any choice that is available on a command menu or in a dialog box.

page break a demarcation that designates where one page ends and another begins.

program a set of instructions or steps, written in a special computer language, that cause a computer to perform a specific sequence of operations or actions.

pull-down menu a menu that appears below the menu bar when selected.

RAM an acronym for Random Access Memory. RAM is a temporary storage area within a computer's active memory that is used to hold and/or change information. It is erased when a computer is turned off.

ROM an acronym for Read Only Memory. ROM is an unalterable set of codes or instructions that are essential for a computer's proper operation and are permanently stored on special memory chips.

ruler a horizontal measure that can be optionally displayed onscreen and that displays special symbols representing tab settings, indention, and margin settings.

save an operation in which information in a computer's RAM is copied to a magnetic disk and assigned a filename.

scrolling the process of moving the onscreen view, functioning as a window, to reveal other portions of a document.

software any application composed of one or more programs that is stored on disk and used for a specific purpose.

system a generic term that refers to a computer and any attached peripheral devices.

toggle a switch that alternately turns an option on or off each time a key is pressed or the option is otherwise selected.

undo an operation that allows the last operation performed to be reversed. An undo operation often acts as a toggle, in which each successive undo toggles between the original version and the changed version.

window the portion of the computer screen through which a document or application tools can be viewed.

Index